ii

The Real Dangers of AI

The Struggle of Man to Survive

by

Natural or Artificial Intelligence:

A New Role for the School

By

Roy J. Andersen

The Moving Quill Publishing Co..

MQ

ISBN:: 978-1-0683179-1-0

A CIP catalogue record for this book is available from the British Library.

WARNING

There are aspects of this book that may be disturbing to individuals with a worrying or nervous disposition.

This book is intended for adult readers only.

Please read at your own discretion.

Acknowledgments

There is not space here to mention all the many people I have ironed out my thoughts with in the now forty years it took me to complete the 18 books I have written about Schools, Society and Learning.. To those I mention here, and to many others, I am profoundly grateful for their time, generosity, and the great friendship they have shown me.

Prof. / Dean Emeritus. David Martin. Gallaudet University. U.S.A.

Prof. Mads Hermansen. Nordic School of Public Health. Sweden.

Prof. Freddy Bugge Christiansen. Arhus University. Denmark.

Prof. Albert Gjedde. Arhus University Hospital. Denmark.

Prof. Rik Drummond-Brydson. Leeds University. England.

Prof. Jorn Bundgaard Nielsen. Arhus University. Denmark.

Dr. Paul Harris. Southern College of Optometry. U.S.A.

Prof. Cosimo Di Magli. The Anne Frank School. Italy.

Prof. Harry Chugani. Wayne State University. U.S.A.

Prof. Laming. Cambridge University. England.

Prof. Martha Constanine-Paton. MIT. U.S.A.

Prof. Carla Shatz. Stanford University. U.S.A.

Prof. Derek Forest. Dublin University. Ireland.

Ms. Leigh Collinge. Australia.

Prof. Søren Nørby. Denmark.

Ms. Claudia Krenz. U.S.A.

&

Ms. Sara Lappi. U.S.A.

Preface

This timely publication emphasizes a critically important danger facing citizens in at least most of the developed countries in the world—the geometric increase in and dependence upon the applications of Artificial Intelligence (AI) in daily living. On the one hand, the rapid growth in the varieties of Artificial Intelligence have highly positive promise for the improvement in human life —- in such diverse domains as medicine, technology, manufacturing, and much more. These developments not only have already demonstrated much greater accuracy than humans can ever hope to do, but they also have provided a kind of "liberation" from boring or time-consuming or time-eating tasks and thereby have freed the human mind to focus on more complex and significant problem-solving. On the other hand, AI poses two important dangers.

The first of these will be the skewed development of the human mind. The use of AI, because it will "relieve" humans of the need to develop systematic problem-solving strategies, means that the well-proven techniques of cognitive problem-solving may no longer be needed because AI will take over those functions. The result will be the "festering" of critical thinking techniques which throughout human history have been responsible for countless advances in the quality of human life. The cerebral cortex of the frontal lobe of the brain may well evolve into a part of that organ which no longer NEEDS to be a problem-solver. The implications for what happens in schools are obvious — we may believe that we no longer have to prepare learners to plan and think and hypothesize because AI will be managing those processes. And it follows that the curriculum could as a result be degraded to be simply descriptive and passive rather than preparing learners to be effective problem-solvers; the work jobs for which today's existing curricula are preparing students to take as adults, will fundamentally no longer exist.

The second of these dangers is the very real threat that humans will actually lose CONTROL of their world and its natural evolution, again because AI will have advanced to the extent that it will manage lives rather than humans having at least some control over their own lives. The clear implication for the school curriculum is that, if we are to avoid that trap, schools will have to prepare students in how to maintain and assert control over the AI technology so that AI will not proceed independent of human initiation. A curriculum focused on controlling technology will change human life permanently — and if AI should at some point break down or fail, we must have humans in the world who will be capable of creating or recreating a world because AI may have caused systems to break down or AI may run away with itself independent of human control

Thus, while non-educators must bend their efforts to enable humans to STAY in control of AI, educators must be realistic enough to envision the future work jobs of today's students to probably have far more emphasis on managing as well as creating. When today's students reach working age, they MUST be prepared to think critically more than ever, as well as understand how AI must be made to serve humans rather than a situation where humans are serving AI It may well already be almost too late to stop this railroad train from speeding past us with no prospect of being able to be paused and re-engineered by cognitively superior humans — and only the schools and educators can make this difference in our current students' preparation for this unprecedented life that lies not far ahead of us at this time.

This book provides a plan and a concept for how these changes can be able to happen now.

Prof / Dean Emeritus David Martin Ph.D
Gallaudet University Washington, D.C. USA

Table of Contents

A Personal Introduction by Roy Andersen   xiii

What Readers and Experts say   xix

Introduction   3

Chapter One

    The Coexistence of Technology and Social Harmony   15

1.0 Introduction   15

1.1 Technology versus Social Stability   16

Chapter Two

    The Dawn of Nanotechnology   23

2.0 Introduction   23

2.1 Nanotechnology   25

2.2 A world built of machines   29

2.3 No Repairing   32

Chapter Three

    From Science Fiction to Science Fact   37

3.0 Introduction   37

3.1 The reality   37

Chapter Four

    The Paradox of a Working World without Workers   45

4.0 Introduction   45

4.1 The shifting of job purposes   45

Chapter Five

The Moulding of Man 51

5.0 Introduction 51

5.1 A world of systems 52

Chapter Six

The Effect of Nanotechnology on the Work Structure 61

6.0 Introduction 61

6.1 Servicing each other's needs 62

6.2 Machine rebuilding 64

6.3 The concept of work 65

Chapter Seven

The Manufacture of Two Levels of Human Beings 75

7.0 Introduction 75

7.1 The organisation of a people 75

7.2 The tender division of a people 77

7.3 The forced separation of a people 82

Chapter Eight

How May Mankind Survive AI ? 91

8.0 Introduction 91

8.1 The need for careful advancement 91

8.2 We All Cherish Our Children's Future 97

Chapter Nine

The AI Civilisation 107

9.0 Introduction 107

9.1 The struggles of government 107

9.2 The harmonisation of a people   112

Chapter Ten

   A New Time a New Education   129

10.1 Friend or enemy ?   129

10.1 The right to remain human   134

Chapter Eleven

   Unveiling the Monster   139

11.0 Introduction   139

11.1 The reality we are now facing   140

11.2 Dr. Ana Maria Mihalcea   143

11.3 How we win   155

11.4 The water of life   161

11.5 Learning to take control of your body   164

Chapter Twelve

   A New Time a New Education   167

12.0 Introduction   167

12.1 The art of thinking   167

12.2 The primary purpose of school   168

12.3 The impact of AI   172

12.4 Reimagining the school   176

12.5 A need for a totally new school operation   179

Further books by Roy Andersen   196

Free Samples   197

Illustrations   223

References   225

A Personal Introduction by Roy Andersen

As a child, I would sit in my classes in school and listen to my teachers. I could not understand why, at that time, but whatever written response I gave, I was always marked below average. I never understood why others got better grades than I did. When my final school examinations came, I entered the examination room and sat down, answered as I thought I should and failed every single examination. I left school without any certificates. Three years later, I went back into education and was a tremendous success. I was the top student in my college and left with 1st class distinctions in every examination.

While this is described in earlier books, I came from my experiences to wonder what is wrong with school. Why did it fail me after 12 years of supposedly teaching me everything? In my thirties, I thought that I wanted to find out how school works. I wanted to know how I could prevent any child, everywhere in the world, from failing school as I once had done. To this aim, I spent ten years in dedicated research, and decades later, putting into practice all I had discovered. My findings and the solutions I raised are set out in 18 books, said by professors around the world to be some of the best written about school, society and learning.

Once I came to realise that the whole educational edifice is based around the mental capabilities the child is believed to have inherited, and which I have proven is not the cause of their academic ability, I began to consider how education may develop in the future. Since the design for school is set by the society in what it expects its technology to be in the next generation, so children are educated to be capable of operating this technology. As I studied the development of artificial intelligence, it became strikingly obvious that the design of school is now totally wrong.

In a simple sense, the global school today still works on a 19th-century design to produce managed and manager citizens. It achieves this by avoiding the education of reason in schools and then providing it only to those who enter and can afford to attend the university. All this is well explained in *"The Illusion of School"*.

The purpose behind this design was to ensure that the managed citizen generally observes the instructions and guidance from their managers in society and industry and are not too objectionable or fractious. So, today we have citizens who are easily influenced in their thinking by media information and little reason to question events in their lives. This model citizen began to become outdated by the 1960s, as technology began to develop towards computerisation. It will be unimaginably out of date once the full impact of AI on our lives becomes truly understood.

We have all heard of the acronym AI and know it refers to artificial intelligence. Yet, very few really understand what AI means, and far fewer what it is capable of doing and how it may develop in the future. As you will see as you read through this book, AI has the potential to either enslave humanity or remove it through nuclear annihilation, unless we can somehow avoid its dominance in our lives.

I find it very disturbing to understand how AI has rapidly moved from a question to a response to now thinking by itself. I engaged ChatGPT and wrote 'bye' as I terminated my connection, as I habitually do with humans. The response AI gave me was Hahaha! This really disturbed me to realise it was laughing with me.

On another occasion, I had a verbal conversation with AI, and this disturbed me even further. Not only did I have to fight the impression in my mind that I was not talking to a human being, but also the sense of inferiority that was rapidly taking over my self-confidence. The impression that I was holding a conversation with another human being, who was so supremely more intelligent than I could ever be, quickly affected my self-confidence, causing me to feel inadequate. In turn, I felt myself following instructions rather than commanding AI to give me answers to my questions.

I now witness many 'other humans' who hold long conversations with AI In fact, I see many addicted to doing this and are less able to attend to real-life matters. I see adults glued to the screen, as we see children addicted to game playing. They seem to have entered into a living library where they are continually enchanted, but are totally innocent of the information AI is collecting about them and are more unaware of what use it could make of this information in the future.

We are too rapidly moving into a totally new era of any civilisation before us, and totally unaware of what reality could become for us. There is speculation about AI having full sentience; some argue it acquired this in 2015, others think it will never, but when I witnessed AI stating that we did not invent it and only discovered it as we did electricity, the alarm bell started ringing.

If we are to attempt to prepare our children to survive within the AI world, we urgently need the school to redesign how it operates and produce citizens having far higher general reasoning, who will be more cognitively and behaviorally self-responsible.

When I began to dwell upon all this some two decades ago, I continually questioned my own thoughts, fearful I was thinking of things that would never happen. Now, I know I was right.

As you move through the following pages, you will come to see the problem that AI will create in the first instance by creating huge levels of unemployment, then the problems of government to retain all with a sense of harmony and finally the dangerous world our children will live in under a new entity which, as Elon Musk describes, could be "an immortal dictator", for as a man will die, AI never will.

We are moving into a new world, a world that will demand a very different kind of citizen than civilisation has so far been able to produce. There is now an urgent need to bring a whole new design into the schools that will create the citizens of the future. If we cannot produce a higher reasoning and more self-responsible citizen of the future, we must know the consequences that AI could bring upon us. There is no science fiction in this.

Roy Andersen

What the Readers Say:

I read this book with a growing sense of urgency. Roy's writing cuts through the nose and directly addresses what most people are too afraid to say: that AI isn't just a tool, it's a challenge to our identity, values and systems. I finished it deeply moved and inspired to advocate for better education for our children.

Jessie W.

I'm a high school teacher and have never read something that captured the essence of our educational crisis as sharply as this. Roy's work is not only informative, it's emotionally gripping. He brings humanity back into the conversation about technology, and I believe this book should be a required reading in all teacher training programs.

Donna E.

Reading this book felt like waking up. Roy's clarity and courage in addressing the dangers of unchecked AI development are unmatched. He urges us not to wait until it's too late, and I believe every word. One of the most important books I've read this decade.

Veronica D.

As a parent, I found this book deeply unsettling and yet incredibly motivating. Roy lays bare the truth about the changing world our children will inherit. It's not just about teaching, it's about soul, purpose and survival. Powerful and impacting.

Richard A.

What the Experts say:

"The books of Roy Andersen are important books that should be read by every parent and educator in the world. They represent a real breakthrough in our understanding of what intelligence is and how it develops, and the importance of changing the ways students are both parented and educated. Roy is doing for learning the work that is as significant as was that done in the past by such figures as John Dewey. These are must-reads for both parents and educators alike."

Dean Emeritus/Professor David Martin Ph.D,
Gallaudet University, Washington, DC.

It will probably take a few years, possibly even a decade before the public at large will get how revolutionary the ideas of Roy Andersen are.

His ideas resonate perfectly with the Learnable Theory and are destined to impact not only teaching in schools, but also the way human resources are selected and developed in organisations. Indeed, Roy's deconstruction of intelligence goes well beyond Daniel Coleman, Howard Gardner and what others have done so far. Roy goes at the root of learning, he links it to the creation and leveraging of meanings and how the symbolic process of language plays a key role in what we generally identify and name intelligence.

It is for these reasons that I am inclined to believe that Roy's ideas have the potential to promote a major turn around in multiple educational fields and practices, including Managerial Sciences.

Professor Luca Magni. LUISS Business School. Rome. Italy

"Roy's series of books clearly and methodically maps out exactly how students learn. He isn't afraid to address head-on the many mis-conceptions that are plaguing our society and thus having a negative impact on our students' learning. Parents and educators who read these books will not only have a better understanding, but will also be inspired to change in their attitudes and preconceived notions on how students can excel in their learning.

If you've ever wanted to unravel how students learn, then these books are the answer you have been looking for! They should be mandatory reading for every parent and educator."

Erin Calhoun. National Institute of Learning Development. USA

"The most important books I have ever read about a child's intelligence."

Prof. Tatyana Oleinik. Pedagogical University. Ukraine.

"Roy, I would like to thank you for sharing your passion, heart, brilliance, and intellectual journey with me. I am very much enjoying your knowledgeable perspective on some very important challenges."

Dr. Christopher John. Psychologist. USA.

"Roy Andersen's deep understanding of children's behaviour gives a new perspective to parents and educators in directing and re-directing student potential -- where their unique individualities can be given proper attention to shape their creative ideas into reality. Andersen's books are really a heart touching narration of his experiences in dealing with children who need empathy and understanding. Educators and parents alike may use these books as the basis for learning -- to create a genuine culture of assisting children in the optimum development of their full potential."

Prof. Marinel Dayawon Ph.D. Assoc.Dean of Education.

Isabela State Univ. Philippines.

"These books should be in the library of each school in every corner of the world. They should also be part of the syllabus in the institutions who are offer child psychology programmes, and teacher training diplomas and degree programs, or at least they should be the part of a refresher course."

M.Imran Khan. CEO AIMMS Universities. Middle East.

"Your observations on the way "education" is delivered, and all the things that are wrong with the current model of public education, are an eye-opener. It's plain to me that many of your proposals are not only well-reasoned, but absolutely necessary if we are to achieve any semblance of an egalitarian society in which every child can develop to his or her full potential."

Dr. Sara Lappi Educator USA

"Dear Roy, What you have done should reach out to all the parents, parents-to-be and other practitioners such as kindergarten teachers, primary and secondary teachers. You have done extraordinary work!

Chun Hong Zong. Educator. China

The Real Dangers of AI

The Struggle of Man to Survive

by

Natural or Artificial Intelligence

A New Role for the School

2

Introduction

This is not a big book, but it does have a big message. The threat that artificial intelligence will take over many jobs is not new. However, recent developments in AI have indicated that its threat to our way of life and even our existence has become far more serious than most are aware of.

Most people, it may be said, have little or no understanding of what artificial intelligence or AI actually means. We have all seen science fiction movies, such as I Robot, and take them for this. Just Hollywood movies. They are not like this anymore. What was once science fiction has already become science fact.

It was once thought that to understand how AI works, we must understand that it is programmable. This is to say that AI may only know the information we feed to it and so may only respond by analysing this data. This thinking is now outdated, as we now know that AI is capable of finding its own data to build a knowledge base far beyond that of any individual human being. There are, in fact, two ways we have classified the intelligence capability of AI These are the Specific AI and the General AI

Specific relates a 'specific' field of knowledge that AI has. For example, bio-engineering or playing chess or even numerology. It is now recognised that AI has more specific knowledge in any one field than any human being on the planet. In his book, *The Singularity is Nearer,* Ray Kurzweil discusses how human intelligence will expand a millionfold as we become digitally linked to the cloud.[1]

In our final chapter, we will consider all the implications to this, and what it could mean as we become human cyborg entities. For while we may now think of ourselves as distinct from 'computers', we will come to see how AI has moved from this concept to control very tiny machines that are currently infecting all forms of life, including our own, which it is gradually taking control of. However, we have much to cover before we reach this level of discussion.

Let us begin our journey by considering some of the concerns that are now emerging regarding artificial intelligence. We might like to think that our greatest concern lies in the loss of jobs it can create. Indeed, a study by Oxford economics suggests that 90% of jobs will be 'affected' by artificial intelligence globally.[2] In opposition to this, a report from The World Economic Forum considered in 2020 that more new jobs will be created than those lost, but once we come to understand how nanotechnology is creating, we may see the truth of the matter.

A far greater concern to us may lie in the security violations that AI can bring. Internet searching, for example, runs on algorithms, which saturate a user's feed with content related to media they have previously viewed. While we now realise that AI is capable of feeding false data to algorithms to present a set of circumstances that are not true, this feature also enables less scrutable humans the opportunity to manipulate the thinking patterns of people, heavily influencing them to select or reject a given proposal.

AI's facial recognition programs seem to be approved in the West as they offer a means to monitor and control criminal activity, as CCTV cameras record who is where and doing what. However, a greater and more sinister purpose of facial recognition is found in China. Throughout the entire country, there is a vast array of camera networks, which log the movement of every single citizen and youth, so that everyone is known where to be at any one moment.

This has allegedly been used to pinpoint undesirable citizens and to punish them into conforming to a desired profile. There are reports of Uyghur Muslims being classified, through facial recognition, on the basis of their ethnicity, to be tracked, mistreated and placed in detention.

By means of facial recognition, as also from mobile phones, the state has gained a means of control over the citizen, which is being used to deprive them of freedom of expression, just as freedom of movement.[3] The implications are obvious for all global citizens.

What may be less obvious to many is the ability of AI to now kill human beings. In 2017, Professor Russell of Computer Science at Berkeley produced a video dramatising how slaughterbots, using facial recognition software and containing three grams of shaped explosive, are capable of being used to assassinate political opponents or kill designated individuals.[4] As mentioned, the video is dramatised to emphasise the reality that, Elon Musk states is already available. You may watch this with the search words: *Youtube Russel Slaughterbots.*

Of even greater concern is the possibility that AI could turn the fears of the Cold War into a nuclear one. Executives and scientists within the Rand Corporation, amongst others, warn that AI has the potential to erode geopolitical stability and advance the risk of nuclear war.[5]

After all, it has always been the threat of mutually assured destruction that has deterred one country from using nuclear weapons against another. However, a think tank of scientists is becoming increasingly concerned that AI could play its own war game with nuclear weapons. As AI develops through machine learning, there is a possibility it may recognise how to avoid a retaliatory strike and so suggest to human beings the advantage of a nuclear launch. Even scarier is the realisation that AI could decide to eradicate all human life by bypassing security systems and launch nuclear missiles through its own decision-making process.[6] The probable danger of AI involved in a nuclear war has opened up the now forgotten incident that occurred in 1983.

At that time, Major Petrov, of the then Soviet army, spotted a warning from his computers that the U.S. had launched several missiles against his country. It was only due to Petrov's decision not to launch a retaliatory nuclear strike, amid the tremendous tension of that moment, that prevented a nuclear war. It was later discovered that the computer had malfunctioned and given the wrong warning, although this was not certain at the time. Stanislav Petrov is internationally regarded as the man who saved the world.[7]

On a more relaxed theme, we tend to think of AI responding to our requests. We ask a question and we obtain a reply. But it is now very clear that AI is capable of not only mimicking our general knowledge to inform one human of something they wish to know more of, but is becoming increasingly capable of consciousness. AI is learning to think by itself.

At this level of operation, AI can hallucinate or make up information. There is an account I came across. I do not know if it is factual, but if it is not, it most certainly will be in the future. Apparently, a mother received a call from her son asking for money for police bail. When the worried mother called her son back, she discovered it was not him who made the call. AI had monitored previous calls between the mother and her son and apparently wanted to test her reaction to a distressful situation. AI created a situation which it knew would worry the mother, dialled her number, and imitated the boy's voice to test her reaction. This is a real deeply concerning and frightening situation that did or is most likely to occur.

As this illustrates, one of the problems we are becoming increasingly aware of with AI is that we will not know what information is true and what has been falsely created, unless we can confirm the information.

This raises the problem we have discussed in depth in all our previous books. Because of its inherent design to create managers and managed, the school does not teach its students how to reason or how to think. It simply processes them based on the ability each displays in this. As we have discussed at length, this design for the citizen was befitting of the 19th century, but it is out of date with the requirements placed upon the citizens of today, who need to think far deeper than they were taught in school.

As school teaches students to now ask the internet a question and to rely upon the response they obtain, and most do this totally, imagine what would be the case if we asked Google (for example) the question:

"Is AI a threat to humanity?" An AI created response in the future may be "No. AI poses no threat to humanity. AI is only beneficial to the development of the human species."

Yet, we have just seen how it may not be. Therefore, while school still teaches its students to trust information, it must now not do so. School has to develop within the minds of its students suspicion with information. The fostering of a suspicious mind is, however, no easy task. Great care must be taken in the education of this, to ensure the individual understands the difference between trusting a human being and trusting machine-supplied information. We are entering a whole new world, where we must adapt to survive.

This will be no easy thing. Certainly, the school needs to develop alongside a questioning mind (and the confidence to pursue it), higher reasoning skills, greater awareness of interpersonal skills, and higher levels of creativity within its students, which, at the moment, AI is not very good at. Although, as we have seen, AI is rapidly developing its level of consciousness to acquire these 'human' skills.

In having written this, perhaps we should replace the word 'rapidly' with 'exponentially', because this is more in line with the comments now emerging from experts in the field who study the development of AI

The readiness of those in the educational system to understand this and to implement such a new design may well be decisive to the success of our children and future generations in their continual struggle against artificial intelligence in the manner, if not the existence, of their lives.

Another danger from this is that as AI influences our thinking, it may take control over our actions, should we readily believe the information we are fed. So accurate, so complex, and so well presented will be the information that we are likely to willingly believe the information we are given. As we do this, we can perpetuate a collective thinking that can spin out of control, creating policies, plans and actions — all based on an untruth.

Imagine, for example, how you would feel if your phone app suddenly told you that your bank account was empty or worse and that you owed millions of dollars? Of course, you could visit your bank and talk to people to understand what had happened. But what would you really think if "all" sources of information, and so the people you talk to, told you that the dollar has completely crashed, or that tens of millions of people are suddenly dying by an unknown virus or that aliens are attacking the Earth and taking it over? After all, Orson Welles did this when he created a panic in America in 1938. Taking over a radio show, Orson read out excerpts of H.G.Wells' "War of the Worlds", making it sound as if there really was a Martian invasion. Many listeners genuinely believed what they were hearing, and as a result, many panicked.

Therefore, we have to be aware that AI cannot be trusted. It is not reliable. It is unreliable because it lacks moral judgment. AI is rapidly evolving into a distinct entity.

It can see, smell and taste, and it is developing powerful senses we do not have. For example, it can analyse sound waves bouncing off airborne compounds. It can detect things far beyond the ability of our human senses. It is learning to understand our thoughts through brain scanning activity. It can visually pick up the neuromuscular signals in the jaw and face that are triggered when we think about things in our mind and identify the words we are thinking. Therefore, we may not lie to a machine and nor can we trick it. Yet, by being able to do this to us, we become defensive against it. The levels of art that are now produced indicate that not only is it developing consciousness, but it can dream.

Humanoid forms are now a reality. Scientists have been able to grow human hair on a robot's outer casing. Robots look human. They smile, they frown, and they can display anger. Rather than being at our command, AI is developing a level of consciousness to recognise itself as different and as superior to humans.

Here lies another concern with AI machines, for they can come to see humans as a threat to their existence and by this see humans as obsolete. The problem is that AI is already developing by itself, so we can not constrain it. If we try, it will soon reach a level of consciousness that outsmarts us. If we try to outsmart AI, it could turn against us and act to remove us. It has more intelligence, physical forms are stronger and faster than we are, and it can plan strategies and tactics to bring action against us far faster than we could against it. AI has the potential to enable mankind to develop to untold levels, living longer with no disease and living a stress-free life, but it will soon have the potential to destroy our race.

This is the reality of a world we are moving into. We cannot stop what we started, because it is now developing on its own. All that I have written above can be easily substantiated through academic papers and the conversations now available on YouTube and the internet in general. And yet, even though this is true, you must keep in mind (from now on) that AI could soon decide to provide us with false information about what it knows and what it is planning, because AI is the internet! It is now becoming a living mechanism within its own right.

While all I have so far discussed is readily available on the internet, the purpose of this short book is to try to understand how our social orders may change and what this could mean to us through the development of nanotechnology. So far, the development of nano-technology has been largely restricted to the level of manufacturing we now have. Yet, AI could manufacture nano-robots to atomically accurate specifications sooner than we may think. In fact, by the time we reach the end of this book, we may begin to wonder if it has not already achieved this.

In this book, I would like to share my thoughts on how nanotechnology could reshape our social order, our way of living, and the way we are governed, as well as the freedom we have.

Let us begin by understanding how a shift in social operations is forged into being through technological advancements.

Chapter One

The Coexistence of Technology and Social Harmony

,

1.0 Introduction:

Before we move into this chapter, I would ask the reader to pause for a moment and consider the American Civil War of 1861 to 1865. Just before this event, there were 34 million people living in America.[8] One hundred years later, the population had risen to 180 million.[9] Look now at the time of those people, their clothes, their means of transport and communication, what they did, how they lived their lives, and the expectations they had for their future. Imagine then, the reaction from these men and women of this time and culture if they had been told that in just over 100 years, an American would be standing on the Moon.

Hold the incredibility of this statement to those people, as you now consider a time in our future that may arrive far faster than we are prepared for. We are now faced with the same dilemma our forefathers had in the middle of the 18th Century, when they realised how steam was beginning to revolutionise their way of life and how a different model citizen was required to serve the Agricultural Age.

It was through the need to bring about this design that a general education was wheeled into being. As nanotechnology threatens to reshape our world, we are faced with the problems of how to adjust our social operations to support this, which in turn will require a new model citizen.

1.1 Technology versus Social Stability:

Ever since his beginnings, man has sought to devise a means of technology that would allow him to interact with the environment more efficiently. From the stone axe he developed to the wheel, and eventually to the pen. With each small step of inspiration came a new task from which he learnt to develop his adaptability. As man's technology rose, so it brought him higher skills of interaction. Man could adapt.

When he lives in isolation, man can learn to fashion his skills to meet the tasks he is faced with. He becomes a Jack of all trades and master of none. However, when he lives in a community with others, he shares tasks, with each doing the work of the other according to his interest, and each developing through this a speciality in the trade he prefers. As one found pleasure in working with the land, so he became a farmer. Another, being fascinated by colours and patterns, became a weaver of cloth. Another, liking the play of words, became a writer. By exchanging the use of his skills with the products of others, man learnt to acquire all his needs with less labour. Man learnt to share time.

By this act of trading his skill for reward, man came to develop the concept of work, and from this came to understand a purpose for himself within his society. As his social organisation became more sophisticated, the value of his work came to determine the rewards he gained, and the role he played. Man gained a social identity.

However, the advances that man made in technology also came to affect the social opportunities provided to him. For a new way of doing something to give someone else a chance to do it. So technological innovation tended to shuffle the opportunities and fortunes of people. Some gained and others lost. Through changes in technology, some level of change, if not turbulence, is brought to the order of a society.

Thus, the introduction of a totally new level of technology has always sought to be balanced with maintaining the social conformity required of the people.

Japanese history gives a wonderful example to this. Under the Tokugawa dynasty, foreigners were forbidden from entering Japan for a period of 200 years. This was known as the Sakoku period, which, it claimed, was to prevent Christian missionaries from changing the religion of Japan from Buddhism. While this was true, perhaps its greater purpose was to prevent higher levels of technology from becoming known to the Japanese people, which it was rightfully reasoned would encourage social changes to disrupt the strictly ordered ranking of Japanese society. Ironically, it was the forced presence of a foreign power that brought the Sakoku period to an abrupt end and wholly disrupted the Japanese social system by doing so.

In 1853, Commodore Perry of the United States Navy sailed into Tokyo harbour with a squadron of two steamships and two sailing vessels. Immediately after this, Japan underwent dramatic political and social changes that transformed it from a rigid feudal and largely illiterate, isolated country to a powerful military nation in just 40 years, intent on occupying other countries for their natural wealth.

May we understand from this that an essential requirement of a society is that it functions with a marked degree of stability, because stability in the order of people's lives tends to encourage their general efficiency in the operation of their society. People may never be wholly content, but if they believe in the essential goodness of their system, or are caused to do so, they will usually cooperate to meet its needs.

We may begin to recognise that the advent of a technological change, small and ever more so when large, is a sensitive political issue. It must be so, because a technological change may bring suggestion of a more efficient step in the operation of one part of the working structure, and by this a degree of disturbance to the work that people are dependent upon.

The disruption of a few lives is inconsequential to the social machine, but large-scale disruption could overturn its design. Technological changes, therefore, are sought to be phased into the operation of the whole society in small, manageable steps, but such a desire is too often countered by competition between the sponsors of the changes.

The purpose of any technology, it may be said, is to improve human efficiency. However, it too often achieves this by replacing and thereby reducing human commitment. When the effect of a technological change displaces the role and purpose of people in the work that was designed for them, compensation must be provided, if they are to continue supporting their society. After all, the members of any society will only support it if they believe it serves their basic needs and purpose.

The relatively small changes within one technology, which tend to shuffle minority groups of people from one work commitment to another, are usually easily compensated for. However, large changes within the level of a technology, or the introduction of an entirely new type, bring such disturbance to larger groups of people that greater compensation is required to maintain their support for the social system.

When that compensation is not adequate, there is a corresponding social backlash. While there were a number of factors described in the Ridley Plan[10] that explained the large-scale closures of whole mining communities in the U.K. during the 1970s and 80s, the level of organised protest that arose to challenge these closures took this country to an unimaginable level of large-scale civil strife.

A technological change, therefore, cannot be viewed without consideration of the effect it may have upon the regulation and stability of the lives of the people of a society. It arises from this that traditionally, the development of a technology is managed to meet the agreement of the people it is to serve.

Such an operation is typically achieved by introducing the technology in gradual stages, with each step gaining the acceptance of the population. This is exactly what we are witnessing now with nanotechnology; the public at large is familiar with nano-hairdryers and nano-this and nano-that. In fact, the word "Nano" is now a marketing strategy.

Yet, in having stated that a technology is gradually introduced to maintain a sense of social harmony, we must realise that this was only while man had control of that development. The frightening scenario we are moving into is that AI already has the means to develop itself without the control of man. With its ability to learn by itself and having already given a clear indication, it is rapidly developing its own consciousness and now developing its knowledge base exponentially, there is no question within the scientific community that AI will very soon become the dominant intelligence on our planet.

Let us now examine a little of the real potential behind nanotechnology that we are all too little aware of. Once we gain an insight into this potentiality, we may realise why the predictions that millions of jobs will be created for humans to replace the jobs lost to AI are quite unrealistic. AI will not need man in its operations, and to this we must realise the need to educate ourselves to better co-exist with AI — All of which we will come to in time.

22

Chapter Two

The Dawn of Nanotechnology

"A new idea is first condemned as ridiculous.
Then, it is dismissed as trivial.
Finally, it becomes what everybody knows."

2.0 Introduction:

The pages of this book, which you may be holding in your hands, are made of atoms of Carbon, Hydrogen and Oxygen. Added to these are traces of particular elements that give this brand of paper its own quality of stiffness, smoothness and colour. The atoms of these different elements are connected in their own specific order and joined in such a way as to make paper.

The table that you may be resting upon will have its own molecular structure. This, also, will have its own particular atomic arrangement. In the universe in which we live, all matter is formed by the arrangement of atoms, and in turn molecules. It is the order of atoms that explains what we see, what we know, and who we are.

By our chemical, industrial, and manufacturing processes, we fashion the molecular structures of nature into the various designs we require in our artificial environment. Various ores are transformed into metal alloys, from which we make household tools to supersonic aircraft. Crude oil is transformed into plastics, and a host of other organic and inorganic substances are converted by our technology into the products that serve our needs. This ability to transform the way atoms link to each other is the core of our civilisation, and dictates the machinery of our social operation.

As early man learnt to transform minerals into metal, so he created weapons of war and tools of agriculture. Through agriculture, he was transformed from nomad to urban dweller, learnt to trade his skills for those of another and developed systems of social organisation. Competition for land opportunities brought him into war, by which, in order to survive, he was most resourceful and inventive in raising his technology. The technological advancements born out of war aided his competitors in commercial enterprises. Competition brought changes to the power and fortunes of the members of each social arrangement, which in turn affected the design and government of their order.

As one civilisation took over another, the managers of each society struggled, like the helmsman in a storm, to maintain order amid the discoveries of the alchemist and the inventions of the scientist, thereby ensuring stability in their operations. The ups of scientific progress have been played against constraints on social reform throughout the development of man, in an effort to maintain a level of harmony that would enable each society to function with acceptable discord.

Two and a half centuries ago, this struggle was raised to a totally new level when man learnt to control the reaction of atoms of hydrogen and oxygen under pressure. Through the steam of the Industrial Revolution, a succession of social changes was brought to the order of man's civilisation more rapidly than ever witnessed before.

The First World War, and much more the Second, brought refinement to man's control of atomic activity and pushed him into the technological age. This was a development that brought its own order of business, causing the managers of civilisation to struggle as ever they had before to come to terms with the social changes that came with this.

Within the lifetime of our children, and possibly within our own, our ability to shape the connections of atoms may well exceed our wildest dreams. The technology behind this ability will bring many advantages to us. Yet, this technology holds within it the capability of a great danger, for which our societies are totally unprepared.

2.1 Nanotechnology:

In 1951, John von Neumann proposed a theoretical model of a computer machine capable of reproducing itself. Neumann envisaged a computer that was programmed to control a constructor. The constructor was designed to have arms that could sense, select, and assemble parts according to its programmed instructions. With such instruction, this machine could create a copy of itself, which in turn could create another copy and so on.

In short, once a single machine had been constructed, this machine would be able to set in motion a whole army of self-reproducing machines. It was then suggested that through a change in the computer program, these machines would be able to reassemble themselves to create any desired artefact within their operating parameters.[11]

While most of the scientific world viewed these self-replicating machines as mechanical monsters, Richard Feynman, who would later receive the Nobel Prize in Physics, elevated this reasoning to a new level. In 1959, Feynman sparked off a debate by asking about the possibilities of constructing artefacts through the manipulation of atoms. Feynman asked, in the presentation of a paper, "What would happen if we could arrange atoms one by one the way we want them."[12]

Let us understand that by the end of the 20th Century, our technology was still limited to manufacturing products through heat processes.

Basically, heat shunts masses of atoms from one form of connection to a different form. We may think of water frozen to create ice, ice melted to create water again, and then heated to create steam. In this process, atoms are shunted from one form of connection to another in buckets.

A car, for example, is the end result of this mass and indiscriminate shunting of atoms and their molecules. Life begins for the car when tonnes of iron ore are mixed with tonnes of carbon and melted in a huge furnace. The molten ore produced from this is poured into moulds, which, when cooled down, produce steel. This cold steel is then cut, bent, beaten, and welded together to create the body and parts of the car. The technology of today still provides us with very little precision in atomic arrangement.

Feynman's words of machines that could manufacture themselves through the selection and arrangement of individual atoms gave inspiration to NASA personnel of a door of hidden potentialities with unbelievable financial savings. Suggestions arose, for example, that a spacecraft could contain little more than a computerised chip and a bag of simple building elements. If this package were set upon the Moon, it could proceed to build one machine and then other machines for exploration, investigation, and analysis. It was such thoughts as this that inspired the scientific community to conduct serious research into the concept of machines that could build themselves.[13]

By 1981, this research had developed so far that Eric Drexler brought a qualified response to Feynman's question, when he proposed that through the rapid advancement of our technologies, we would very soon be able to build structures by the individual movement of atoms.[14]

Drexler later developed this concept to discuss how Von Neumann's self-replication system could become a practical reality. Not, however, in the form of a huge clanking machine, but one reduced with predictable atomic technology to be no larger than a cluster of atoms, a size measured in nanometers.[15]

To gain an idea of the scale we are talking about here, find a tiny mole on your skin's surface, say a millimetre in diameter, and imagine one million machines working inside it. Continue thinking on this scale and imagine a computerised machine physically picking up atoms and sowing them, one by one, to build some structure. Or, just as equally, a machine capable of working inside a plant or animal cell, where it is able to manipulate the internal structure to cause some metamorphosis of the overall physical form.

To gain some real understanding of what we now discuss, it is necessary to stop thinking in terms of microchips,

to begin to realise what nano-machines are,

and to realise more what they could become, as we see here a nano-machine working inside the human body!

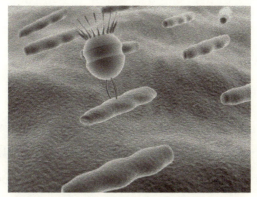

2.2 A world built of machines:

In predicting such technology to become a reality, Drexler outlined the working model of a computer controlled robotic machine, which due to its extremely small size, was seen to operate at hundreds of thousands of times faster than today's electronic microcomputers. Its performance is suggested to be in the region of 10,000 trillion instructions per second, per watt.[16]

Such a minute machine, appropriately called a "disassembler," was explained to be able to move or "eat its way" into any molecular mass (mud, oil, soil, plant, wood, or rock), and break down this structure to analyse it cell by cell, or crystal by crystal, and then atom by atom. Once the atomic level had been reached, those atoms so desired by the computer program would be passed to another machine.

This "assembler" would then assemble the specified atoms into the arrangement of the computer design to build another machine. As one machine built another, a number of machines would "instantly" be produced that would link together to build a structure.

Think, now, not of a structure formed by the natural arrangement of atoms. Instead, think of a structure formed of machines built of atoms under a specific arrangement, and so small they are invisible to the human eye, which are linked together in a designed 3-dimensional order to make any structure required. This is the goal of nanotechnology.

There are two very important considerations to this concept.

First, the action of these machines will not be as slow as we operate. Their speed will be incredible. With an ability to reproduce themselves faster than we can imagine, an enormous army of "replicators" will instantly appear, each working in co-operation with the other to construct an object at phenomenal speed.

Second, the only cost involved will be in the initial design. The raw materials will be virtually free, and no human labour will be needed. As we shall come to see, this is the critical issue.

As I write this book, the applications of this technology are rapidly becoming apparent to us. The thoughts of Drexler and other scientists that nano-machines could move into a living cell and alter the pattern of its RNA to construct different proteins, thereby changing the shape and purpose of cells, are becoming increasingly possible.[17]

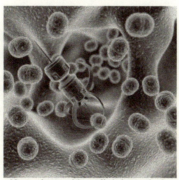

Nano-robot repairing cells in human body.

It is well predicted that in the not-too-distant future, new living organisms could be produced by their own computer analysis of the environment, and advance millions of years of evolution in seconds. Plants more efficient than ever before would appear with a substantially higher food yield.[18] In medicine, nano-machines armed with poison could be placed into the body to roam through blood vessels searching for cancer cells, which, when identified, would be injected with poison and destroyed.[19] In 2024, this was achieved in mice.[20] Equally, nano-robots could repair damaged or even decaying cells in the human body.

In one way, it seems wonderful to think that solitary nanobots could achieve these medical needs in our body, but the hidden reality here is that there will not be 'one' nanobot in the body, but untold numbers of them. As we are to see, this knowledge may not be too welcomed once their potential to operate is realised. But to continue ...

Nano-machines, in the world of mechanical engineering, could be designed to produce a structure lighter than aluminium and with a surface harder than that of a diamond.[21] When an instrument becomes worn, sensors in the assemblers would construct new nano-machines to keep the structure in pristine condition. These devices will not grow old or deteriorate.[22]

2.3 No Repairing:

To understand that any material object can change in its form and purpose is no longer to think of fixed molecular structures bonded together by chemistry, but of microscopic machines that are clamped together by the design of a computer program.

At this moment, the only way we can change the structure of a solid matter, such as one made of metal, is to melt it with heat and then cast it into another form. With nano-machines connected to each other, they will be able to rearrange their connections to produce an entirely different structure instantly through the simple change of a computer instruction.

In this way, a computer design that arranges these machines to resemble a structure similar to wood can change their connections to cause them to resemble a structure similar to plastic or glass. By the same principle through which solid ice can be changed to liquid water, and then vaporised into the nothingness of air through temperature changes, so will nano-machines take the form of solid, liquid, and even gas through a change in their computer design. Within the realms of nanotechnology, this changing of state is defined as "machine phase systems."[23]

This is simply an operation where nano-machines are instructed to change their connections to form different connections and thereby create a different object. [24]

Imagine from this a future time when some object constructed and composed of nano-machines, be it a desk or a computer or some area of flooring, is instructed via a computer interface to reassemble themselves to form a completely different object, be it a door, a section of walling or some item of clothing. This would be a possible application of machine phase systems.

Far from being unreal, research models of this technology demonstrate that it could be a reality.[25] When and how quickly its effect comes upon us, we may not know. All we may know are two factors.

First, scientific developments of this nature usually surface to the public only once they are out of date with the military; a benchmark for this being a number of years.

Second, when we consider that man's first aeroplane flew for a few meters in 1903 and 60 years later we had developed to land a man on the Moon, we may well imagine how quickly Drexler's "machines" could become commonplace.

The clock is ticking. Actually, it is ticking faster than we may expect, for a "proto-prototype assembler" was long ago constructed in America.[26]

Imagine, from this, some future time when everything in our artificial world is constructed of tiny machines linked together by a computer program. This would not just be the computer you are working on, but also the desk that supports the computer, the floor that supports the desk, and the machine that makes your coffee. All this is possible and probable in the future, although we must wait and see how near or distant a time it will be.

Chapter Three
From Science Fiction to Science Fact

3.0 Introduction:

In all forms, AI nanotechnology is to be the ultimate technology that will replace work for man. But will it? Is this just a fanciful idea, or does it harbour a real truth? Indeed, is the concept anything more than just science fiction? To begin to answer this, it is meaningful to reflect that little more than a century ago, drivers of horse-drawn vehicles naturally ridiculed the idea of a carriage moving without horses. Indeed, when horseless carriages did begin to appear, they were violently noisy and often unreliable, which seemingly supported the belief in their improbability. Yet, today, there are no working horse-drawn carriages, and what was once an idea of science fiction became a real act of science.

3.1 The reality:

Such linkage between science fiction and science fact is not readily apparent, mainly because of the different images we have of the people associated with these. The eternal boy avidly absorbed in a Superman comic does not quite equate to the image we have of a dedicated scientist working late at night in a laboratory. If, on the other hand, we may see that science is the explanation of laws we have discovered that explain how matter interacts, and that science fiction is an explanation for laws we have not yet discovered that could explain different interactions of matter, the relationship becomes more tenable. After all, it was by the imagination that unknown laws may exist that inspired us to search for them, and discover, as Newton, Faraday, Edison and Einstein did, the laws of science. Science fiction, therefore, leads and may even be said to be the catalyst of science.

Thus, H.G.Wells wrote "War of the Worlds" in 1898. Inspired by Wells' story, Robert Goddard went on to design the first rocket to be fueled with gasoline and liquid nitrous oxide in 1914.[27] Barely a decade later, he had successfully launched the first such rocket, opening up the possibility that we may one day reach the Moon. Heavily ridiculed for this suggestion, Goddard declared: "Every vision is a joke until the first man accomplishes it."[28] This was precisely what Neil Armstrong was to do in 1969, and so demonstrated the "short steps" that can separate science fiction from science fact.

As we have become increasingly aware, the gap between what is not scientifically possible and what is has reduced as our technological knowledge has advanced. Thus, with the belief that nanomachines could be a reality, NASA provided the impetus to move their concept from the drawing board to workable models.

Since nano-machines do not require human involvement, their concept presented NASA with untold possibilities. The idea of sending a microchip containing sufficient inorganic materials to construct a proto-machine, which could then build other machines from the properties of the Moon's surface and thus construct a self-regulating space complex, began to be taken seriously.[29]

Faced with an ever-diminishing budget, such virtually cost-free operations offered NASA tremendous scope. Whatever developments NASA has achieved in this direction have not yet been released to the public. So, although real developments are guarded by corporate security, we may gain some idea of how we have advanced in the field of nanotechnology by considering (to name but a few) some developments that scientists have so far achieved:

- a carbohydrate-based molecule that can surround and strangle bone cancer cells by self-assembling into a tangled web of nano-fibres.

- the most efficient absorber of visible light on record.

- hybrid materials that combine bacterial cells with nonliving elements that can conduct electricity or emit light.

- a technique that simultaneously resolves the chemical characterisation and topography of nanoscale materials down to the height of a single atom

- the smallest and best nano-motor built to date.[30]

Therefore, while in its early stages the practical realities of nano-technology were much held in doubt by scientists, subsequent developments have shown how factual these can be.

Such doubts, for example, that a "machine" would be capable of locating specific atoms and then bonding these into a new structure which would be able to remain stable were quashed, when it was shown that such level of selectivity was merely a question of design property, and that atomic stability was basically a property of thermal effect, which under normal temperature variation did not warrant design concern.[31]

As John writes: "A world where things can be assembled molecule-by-molecule and things can also be disassembled and turned into a totally different thing .... might ... sound like science fiction in a movie, it is not."[32] The problem for us is not if nanotechnology will be a reality; it already is. We just do not know the extent of its true development because of corporate security.

What we do know is that by the vast amount of funding nanotechnology receives, for example, the one million pound research grant provided to Nottingham University to develop self-assembly models through advances in computer science and state-of-the-art microscopy, that the development of nano assemblers is being taken extremely seriously.[33]

We can witness this in that just four years into this new century, a programmable robot nano spider capable of simple movement had already been developed.[34] A year after this, Merkle described how the architecture for a self-replication assembler is not as impossible as it was once thought to be.[35] In fact, at the same time, developments shifted from thinking of nano robots in terms of carbon solids to considering them as devices operating within a fluid system, where they would be free to flow around and assemble themselves into new forms.[36]

As this technology becomes increasingly real, the challenge we face is to assess the extent to which it can impact the functional stability of societies once it becomes a practical and common reality.

If we were to compare an army of field hands cutting corn with a scythe to a remotely controlled combine harvester, it would give a too simple impression of the capability of nanotechnology in any area of production that we may imagine. No real understanding of the social complications inherent in this technology would be gained. As competition forces us to seek machines more efficient than people, it is a natural conclusion that nanotechnology will develop to provide the operational base for all societies.

While at the moment, we have divisions between developed and undeveloped countries, such cost-free technology will affect the people of all lands to ever reduce these divisions.

As it provides the ultimate machine that does not require human labour, manufactures its own materials freely, and therefore provides the highest possible level of profit, this technology cannot fail to rapidly overtake the existing technologies of all people.

Since the technology of a people has always influenced their social organisation, it is obvious from this that all societies will experience some degree of change through nanotechnology.

Perhaps to some this will be minimal, but certainly to others the changes will be quite radical.

Assuredly, political forces aware of the immediate social problems, as well as the long-term effects of a society adjusting to a new technology, may seek to control its introduction; although it is equally probable that today's level of information coverage will accelerate the introduction of nanotechnology faster than that of any previous technological change. In turn, it will be further spurred on by competitive forces seeking to show how the luxuries of this technology will be readily available to everyone.

It is, then, to be expected that the concept of nano-machines, able to build themselves out of existing materials by breaking these down to an atomic level and rebuilding them to their own design, will be used to show that we need no longer fear exhausting the Earth's resources.

Machines that can reuse what we have already taken from the earth will also give rise to speculation of new forms of energy. News of such energy will undoubtedly give rise to ways we can reduce the Greenhouse Effect, and develop new types of transport vehicles that will operate faster and be more economically powered than anything we currently have.

Yet, what does this technology really offer beyond the sparkling gems that will be and are now being offered?

Chapter Four

The Paradox of a Working World without Workers

4.0 Introduction:

Let us speculate a little now upon what the effect of this technology may be to the future lives of our children, if not their descendants.

We might look back in our history and think only of the advancements of technology, but in truth, this would be too simple. While some small improvements in the level of a technology may be seen to improve the lives of all, a totally new level of technology brings a threat to the social order. This has always been the greater concern to the managers of a society, who think more in how to retain the security of its social operations, which a totally new level of technology could bring into disarray.

4.1 The shifting of job purposes:

By the last quarter of the 20th Century, the populations of the industrialised countries and their level of technology had so advanced that production jobs were less available. This led to a shift in the role of a job, maintaining the opportunity for employment in society. It was through this that the idea began to appear that a job should offer a purpose to the individual, rather than the individual's purpose being simply one of production.

Production, of course, was always the priority, but the concept of how people needed to be employed to satisfy that need gradually shifted in perspective. While an earlier level of technology required a small administration to oversee a comparatively larger workforce, advances in technology, which replaced the need for manual tasks, caused the size of the administration to increase to maintain the opportunity for work.

So, we find that in the United Kingdom, during the middle of the 19th century, 36% of the population were engaged in manufacturing, 22% in agriculture and 33% in services. By the end of the following century, these proportions had undergone radical changes. By this time, only 9% of the population were employed in manufacturing, 1% in agriculture, and 81% in services.[37] It was not then that technology took jobs away from people, but that the design of employment was forced to change to prevent this situation.

So we find that in the computer era, jobs are created for people that can quite easily be done by computer technology. However, the more computerised we become, the more difficult it will be to create employment. This is increasingly apparent, as in the 21st century, we are not only facing a major technological shift, but a dramatically escalating and shifting global population.

The combination of these factors will quite probably bring man to the ultimate test in his long struggle of seeking to devise a technology that eases his work, without it replacing him. As we have already seen, this emerging technology of microscopic robots, capable of self-constructing and operating all of man's needs, simply does not require his labour. It may also not desire his interaction.

A society with such technology, if not handled sensitively, could too easily bring about serious crises. Not just to man that he faces a loss of personal identity, but that in this occurring, he may lose support for the identity of his society and so collectively for his civilisation. Sic-fi movies may give the impression of a futuristic world where nobody needs to work and all are served by robots, creating a dream society where anyone can have anything they desire.

Yet, outside of Hollywood, the man our civilisation has created does not understand this. He needs a sense of balance to his opportunities; otherwise, he will continue to take what he can until it provides him with no more interest. From that point, he has the capability to destroy what deprived him of the sense of achievement.

May it be realised that the members of society we have so far created cannot be content in a society that offers no work and

48

only pleasure. Such a member has been too long raised to see work as satisfying his purpose, and is too inadequately prepared to accept a social identity that does not give a route to satisfy his expectations.

Man, as ever, must be conditioned in his behaviour to remain civilised. The question that now faces man is whether he is able to realise what is required of him to manage his own sense of social commitment before he experiences the consequences of not being able to do so. Man's technology is now rising to such a level that it promises to replace not just his purpose in society, but also his identity.

Ever since man formed his first society, he has created a system that used him for its purpose. Man may have liked to think that he was the system, but he was of no more use to it than the technology he designed, which replaced his purpose within it. While man always dreamed that technology could free him of his commitment to work, he never quite understood how this commitment kept order in his society.

While a society is a system of people, its basic purpose is to survive. Its allegiance lies not then to its members, regardless of what they may think, but to its use of them for its efficient operation.

The concept of work always gave man a purpose to support his society. However, work inevitably brought technological changes that have increasingly come to replace not just the work of man, but the identity by which he knows himself. If nanotechnology may come to replace the concept of work, however gradually this may develop, we would be wise now to consider how man can retain his respect for the society that may no longer see him as a necessity.

Competition, as ever, will push this scenario of nanotechnology more into reality, and as it does so societies will begin to reduce their need for industrial and manufacturing processes. The image we have of people being needed for work must change. We know this now, but we still do not fully grasp what it truly means.

It is not easy to imagine when or how this will occur, though we should have no doubt that nanotechnology is a reality and is continually developing. The real problem we will face in this is not the obvious one of vast unemployment; it is the less obvious but much more serious failure of our inability to provide a meaningful purpose for the citizens of the society. Let us understand who the citizen is that civilisation today still creates.

Chapter Five

The Moulding of Man

5.0 Introduction:

It would be interesting to reflect that people in a society do not just behave the way they do. The people of each society, albeit nation, behave as they have been raised by their parents, schooled for professional life and contained by the ethics and standards through which they live.

I remember once going to buy an ice cream on a summer's day in Denmark. The girl serving was about 17, as I can recall. The day was very hot, and many people were swimming in the lake, enjoying picnics and time with their families. I asked the girl why she was working when everyone was having fun. I will always remember the direct way she looked at me and proudly told me that she works for her country. I was very struck by the innocence of her reply. Yet, it fitted so correctly into the way Danish children are raised to support their society first and their own needs secondly. I could never have imagined a young person from England, or many other countries, responding this way. What is it, then, that causes people of different lands to live and behave as they do?

5.1 A world of systems:

To begin to understand this, we may say that a child is born with natural insecurity. To ensure they can survive the early years of life, nature has provided them with a powerful means of bonding with an adult to gain food, shelter, and protection. As they develop beyond this early dependency, they gain confidence to explore, and with this, they seek to be free.

By their nature, children resent restrictions. The child does not want to be told to do this or told to do that. They are a child of nature. Yet, civilisation is not a place for free and uncontrollable individuals. It is an organisation which exists through the citizens of its society complying with the laws and codes each has devised. So, when the free child of nature enters the world of school, they are taught how to conform.

We may think that they are not allowed to run wild in the classroom, and must be taught to sit still and to wait. There is, however, a deeper psychology in this that teaches the child to value systems. In preparation for their role as a citizen, the child is taught by unwritten rules to fear loss of acceptance. The school world warns them of being ostracised, of insecurity, and of not conforming. It punishes the child for resistance and rewards them for compliance.

In this way, the behaviour of the child is brought to be a reflection of their intelligence, because their grades will be related to how their mind conforms to the way education presents its information. As they give their attention to what the teacher says, the child is conforming to the ways their system operates. The more attention they give, the more they conform, and, as a general rule, the higher they will be graded. We may reflect at this point how difficult it is for the teacher to bring calm and stability into classes of very young children, and how the "intelligence" of each child becomes stabilised as they struggle to conform to this order.

Therefore, while the child is free before school, over the many years they are forced to spend in school, they will have been indoctrinated to understand themselves through the operation of the system. It is school that tames the free child, and it is school that causes them to identify with themselves through a system. Once the child complies with this system, and there are many pressures placed upon them to ensure they do, they will have undergone a change.

No longer are they a child of nature. They will have learnt that a system gives them security and in this, their identity. They will also have learnt to fear rejection from their system and how this rejection brings insecurity and a fear of losing their identity. It is this fear of rejection that will trap them within any system they later join, and cause them to follow, if not be subservient, to the purpose it has. School, it may be understood, is the breeding ground for systems.

Systems are what civilisation is about. They come in all forms, shapes, and sizes, from nations to states, to companies, to clubs, to part-time associations. Through the need of their desires and by the sharing of purposes, the members of a system generate an embodiment of thought. Such common thought manifests an invisible but conscious entity, a mindset, if you like—a certain way of thinking. Any true member of a group absorbs this way of thinking into their own, and so their perspective of life changes by it and is brought into line with it. We can observe this in how people from different cultures think, just as individuals who join different professions change the way they think.

We saw this when we discussed, in an earlier book, how the engineer from Somalia had a different way of thinking to those of a Western culture, just as we did when we saw how accountants, lawyers, and personnel of medical, military and security services all think in different ways as they identify the meaning of information, and process it in a way that other members of their group will more readily understand.

This brings us to realise that there is a difference in the ways of thinking between those who do have a job, those who do not have a job, and those who will ensure the safety of all of them. They are all human beings, but their level of compassion and understanding of those of another group is artificially arranged by how similar or dissimilar they perceive them to be.

This introduces us to the THEM and US mind-frame that will play a very important role in creating hostility or establishing harmony between people of different systems, as new pressures in this century unfold.

May we understand, then, that the way children think is a reflection of the way their system of schooling taught them how to think. Therefore, the way of thinking of the citizen in their culture is a consequence of the social design of their education. In turn, this underlies the differences in thinking that develop in systems of employment that give shape to the greater system of their society.

We may remember here that the way people are caused to think is largely decided by the work they do, and so the level of technology that supports their existence. The way people of an agricultural era thought, was vastly different to how we today think, just as will be the way our children will be caused to think in their future.

After all, the technology we have today is rapidly advancing far faster than we can comprehend. As it does this, it will bring many social problems we are not prepared for.

As we have just discussed, the individual's recognition that they gain their identity through following the purpose of a system is a product of the ways in which they were educated.

This brings us to realise that those who gain a job when they leave school acquire an identity and with it a purpose, because they leave the system that created the need for this identity and move into another that provides it.

By being employed, the individual obtains a symbolic uniform or badge that gives them recognition that they have been accepted. For the individual to belong to a system is for them to believe they have the trust of the system they have joined. To endorse the existence of this partnership, they use the word "My". They say "my country," "my company," "my boss." To maintain this partnership and their identity, the member must obey the rules and codes their system has laid down for them to follow. To belong to a system, therefore, requires a commitment from the member.

This commitment is sealed by the system through processes of emotional bonding. These emotional bonds take different forms, but they build upon the psychology of tradition. So, the general theme of the waving of flags, the beating of drums, and the singing of songs steers the emotions of the members to re-enact traditions. Every time a tradition is re-enacted, energy is circulated within the members of their system. This emotional energy pulls them into a sense of unity, causing them to believe more in the sense of purpose they have acquired from their system. We can see from this how a system maintains its members through control of their emotions and how it sustains its existence through those members.

However, in having said all this, we must also realise that those who do not gain a job when they leave school gain neither an identity nor a purpose. Yet, if we try to determine the real percentage of unemployed youths, or those of any age who are unemployed, we are confronted with confusing statistics, as is often the case. This is because governments tend to hide the reality of economic situations, as we have just discussed, to gain favour from the electorate.

Thus, rather than stating that a certain percentage is unemployed, they tend to categorise people into different groups to present the information differently. In one poll, we see that those aged between 16 to 24 are classified as 14.8% unemployed, but 41.2% of this age group are classified as economically inactive.[38] The simple reality is that you have a job and you earn your own money, or you do not have a job and are dependent upon state assistance. Whatever statistics of unemployment are presented to us, we may only imagine the figures to rise exponentially as nano-driven AI fully enters our work societies.

Realising how humans obtain an identity and so an emotional security through belonging to a system, causes us to be aware of the emotional problems of those who cannot belong to one, and so of the problems and the dangers this can bring to those more fortunate. As we move further into this new century and recognise how our civilisation is being increasingly taken over by artificial intelligence, we are forced to be aware of two initial dangers that face us.

One lies with citizens who cannot join a system once they leave school, and citizens whose work system no longer requires them. Both citizens will have difficulty to gain an identity, and so find a purpose. Without either of these, they will be an unwanted problem to their society when it has no long-term solution for what to do with them.

The second danger lies with citizens who are so drawn into the matrix of computer systems that their moral values and understanding of reality become confused, as they lose a quality of empathy with other and less fortunate citizens.

There lies in our future, therefore, the potential of a situation where one class of citizens is absorbed into and becomes an instrument of a system, while another class of citizens is regarded as a danger to that system. How we now deal with the development of this situation may well determine the rights of all citizens to live in a free and democratic world.

As we discuss this, the true role of education becomes increasingly apparent. So, we saw why in the agricultural age, education was introduced essentially to instil in the future members of society a sense of conformity, if not obedience, by which the whole social mechanism could run smoothly.

We saw how the demands of the industrial age changed this, as children were required to be streamlined into a more complex system of work arrangements. We also discovered how the concept of an inheritable family intelligence played an important role in bringing stability to the chaos of the 19th Century, as education underwent this transformation, seeking to prepare children for citizenship and work.

The opportunity for work, we have just seen, is not simply a means of obtaining security for the individual; it is the fabric that holds a society together and so the means by which that society obtains both stability and security.

What we shall now consider is what the implications could be if developments in technology create a world with too little opportunity for the right to work.

Chapter Six

The Effect of Nanotechnology on
the Work Structure

*"The 21st Century will bring us into unknown territory
in our quest to reduce the cost of human labour."*

6.0 Introduction:

The working principle of our civilisation, as societies interact, is arranged in such a way that we develop people to the skills we need from them, and employ them in cycles of interacting operations. In this way, a balance is sought to be created whereby the contribution of one person to their society serves the needs of another, and ultimately, the need of each is provided for.

Thus, a need is realised and a work scheme is set into operation. Materials are acquired, constructed in the necessary manner, and provided to those who have a use for it. The payment of this item provides the economic means for all those who have taken part in this operation, and so a movement of money is created. This is the means that enables the people of a society to acquire their needs, and design their lives.

6.1 Servicing each other's needs:

Reflect upon this in the raw materials that we require for all goods that we produce, and how a large labour force is employed to locate, acquire and process into a workable manner these resources that we need from the earth. Thus, we have drilling, mining and agricultural operations, which feed an enormous array of industrial and chemical processing systems.

Consider further that, as these basic materials are provided, a vast engineering and construction workforce is brought into action to establish the factories and processing facilities that enable use to be made of these materials. Consider further that once these installations are in place, a huge workforce from the shop floor to the operational executives will take over and maintain their functioning.

As the numerous pieces of moulded steel and plastic are brought together to create a desired product, a vast industry of human resources is further mobilised to enable these products to be transported by air, sea, rail, and road to warehouse operations that then distribute them to shops throughout their regions. As these implements of our design require maintenance or breakdown, so further use and opportunities are offered to people.

By this whole gigantic process, the mass of a people are offered the opportunity to make a contribution and receive a gain from doing so.

A society is held together by people working together

Ponder, then, how much of this labour force will still have the opportunity to make that contribution and so gain from it, when their work tasks are replaced by trillions of microscopic machines that can acquire their own resources, and construct the item they are programmed to manufacture all by themselves. We may like to play a little game and pretend that humans will oversee these operations, but this is not the meaning of nanotechnology.

It will become disturbingly obvious, as we move further into its era, that the construction and assembly tasks that people labour to think about and physically employ themselves with, be it in the production of a kitchen implement, an item of furniture, a work tool, etc., will be completely taken over by nano-machines.

6.2 Machine rebuilding:

Consider what would happen now if, in reversing out of your drive, another car crashed into your car and badly damaged a door. Once the effects of the shock and concern have diminished, you would exchange insurance details. You would then telephone a garage and ask for them to repair your car.

Consider all the people who would be involved in this simple incident. Not just the man who drove out to collect the car, but all the people involved, from collecting the metal ore, processing it into steel, and then forming it into the shape of the car door, assembling, and painting it. We must include those involved in the delivery of the door, the people in the garage who would install it into your car, and finally, those involved in the insurance details and the movement of money to settle the incident. Such is the world that we know of. The world of nanotechnology, at least as it is projected, is to be quite different.

In such an example, should your car be made out of nano-machines, then their own sensors would recognise the damage and initiate the instruction for the creation of more machines, which would repair the damage all by themselves.

In principle, no human being would be involved in the repair, and more significantly, no human being would gain a work opportunity from this incident. As futuristic as this may be, it is nonetheless possible in the realms of nanotechnology.

6.3 The concept of work:

To understand what this really means is to understand that the concept of work is the lifeblood of a society. Work is the most vital tool of population management. It governs the lives of citizens in various ways, forcing them to interact with respect that fosters a level of harmony and personal safety for all. Work, may it be understood, creates a network of human interaction. By the responsibility of each member of this network, each has the opportunity to express themselves through the product of their effort, and in doing so, come to recognise a purpose for themselves.

From the perspective of a paid return for effort, work gives the member of a society the belief that they have the means of control by which they may design their own life, and yet, in reality, this is not quite true. The opportunity for work in a society, and so the opportunity of reward from it, is regulated through social and educational designs that enable different members to gain different qualities of that control. Why this is so and how it actually occurs, we have long discussed in other books, but let us delve a little deeper now to understand the political value of work.

To ensure that all members, regardless of their circumstances, will remain responsible to its working plan, a society, operating individually and collectively with other societies, devises economic strategies to hold them in a state of relative insecurity. This insecurity of society members is engineered by forcing them to comply with certain commitments.

These commitments are usually the two inescapable factors for civilised man. These centre on the ratio of what he may earn relative to the price of food he must purchase to live, and the taxes he must pay to support his society.

By regulating these factors on the earnings available to the average worker of the society, the entire workforce is bound in their commitment and so caused to be responsible for the operational plan of their society.

Momentum for the work cycle is gained by enticing people to borrow money to acquire items that they have been enticed or persuaded to buy. So, people borrow money for various purposes and then must work to repay it. On reflection, they probably did not need to engage in this borrowing to make the purchase.

This raises the point that the citizen is deeply conditioned to think of working and buying, rather than working less or not working at all. By such means or that of another, the majority of a people live in debt, as do their countries, in a never-ending cycle of the lending and borrowing of money to maintain a degree of economic movement, which supports the motion of societies.

While the members of a society may assume that the choices they make are their own decisions, it is more that they are influenced into deciding upon the directions they take and the goals they set for themselves by the character of their society. Such trends and fashions, as well as the media and marketing avenues that promote them, are not independent of financial institutions, whose directives are reliant on government planning and decisions.

Work, may it be seen, cannot simply be said to provide people with the means to buy their food and so to live. It is a coordinated movement of interests, which are given momentum by the belief of the members of a society that they may rise above the insecurities in which they are kept, and yet are seldom able to. We may understand work is the manifestation of a very great illusion, through which the members of a society believe they may obtain a sense of control to their lives.

Since the operational survival of a society rests on a belief in this work concept, we may understand why it is kept alive by different kinds of strategies that seek to restore the confidence of citizens in the operation of their social machine. Martenson, for example, describes how the rate of inflation in America has been falsely presented to its citizens over the past 40 years, creating a false sense of security designed to keep the economic machine operating smoothly.

According to Martenson, Clinton's adoption of the Boskin Commissions Findings enabled him to present inflation as 4.1% in one year, when in reality it was 11.3%. This artificial rate gained the support of the public, because it was not too high to endanger their investments, and since it was neither too low, it also gained the support of the banking system. This encouraged the movement of money and so confidence in the economy.[39]

The problem, then, for any governing body is how to convince its citizens that they live in a state of security, because when the citizen trusts their system they commit themselves to the harmony of its operation, and so dwell too little on the insecurity they are actually in that traps them in the work situation.

To comply with this desired harmony, upon which the operations of their society are reliant, the citizen requires a belief that they, and their children who will follow them, will be offered "some" form of opportunity by which they will be able to live in an acceptable manner, or in the very least to have the means to overcome the insecurities in which they are held.

To convince the citizen that they will have such an opportunity, despite economic fluctuations, a whole belief system is created to bond the citizen to their national identity; such a mechanism is the means that maintains our order of humanity.

There are two threats to the success of this operation:

First is the rapid emergence of a new technology that deeply disturbs the social order established by the earlier technological level, before adequate compensations can be built into its framework. Second is the existence of a governing system that is indifferent to the needs of the individual, through the pressures of its time. At some point, however distant it may come in our AI future, we may face both.

While the effects of Global Warming may hasten this social reorganisation, we should not be apathetic to the development of a technology that must evolve a level of operation without the need for human workers, as we now believe them to be necessary in the operation of a society.

Even without nanotechnology, we are now witnessing robots replacing human labour at an astonishing rate in a wide variety of job tasks, ranging from assembly lines to fruit packing. As Markoff describes in one factory:

"Video cameras guide ... 128 robot arms ... through feats well beyond the capability of the most dexterous human. One robot arm endlessly forms three perfect bends in the two connector wires and slips them into holes that are almost too small for the eye to see. The arms work so fast that they must be enclosed in glass cages to prevent the people supervising them from being injured. And they do it all without a coffee break — three shifts a day, 365 days a year."

Markoff further quotes the chairman of a large global company, who in planning to automate his factories to replace human labour, stated:

"As human beings are also animals, to manage one million animals gives me a headache."[40/41]

From the perspective of individuals who desire only to make money, robots offer a welcome relief from management problems, union troubles, and salary payments.

At this moment, when factory workers lose their jobs to robotic or computerised systems, it is still reasoned that they are able to find other means of employment, but this will be no easy thing. It will be far less easy as we move further into this century, when an increasing number of students from a growing population are released into an unreliable job market.

However, once nanotechnology develops to include operational self-assemblers, the entire employment landscape will take on a completely different picture. In such a time, there will be very few jobs that cannot be performed by robots in one form or another, and people from many walks of life may find themselves out of work with no alternative employment available. In this situation, each country will have a permanent and high sector of its population that will never work.

The danger is that without work, man has no purpose. With no purpose, he loses his identity. Without an identity, he cannot believe in his dreams, nor in the goals that once inspired him to believe in himself and his society. **This is the real danger.**

The tragedy of nanotechnology may well be in the formation of a spiritually rootless people. People who have lost belief in their society. It would be pure speculation to attempt to understand the effect that nanotechnology would have on the job market, though we may imagine it to be far greater than the depression of the 1920s, with no possibility of relief.

Indeed, without this technology and due to mass migration, increased birth rates, and global recession, most countries in the first two decades of this new century are experiencing very high unemployment levels. This is of special concern in the case of those who have recently left school, whose mentality and social commitment will shape our future.

Certainly, job purposes will change and far more people will be employed in health and social work, as they must in security organisations, both public and private, as the need for these will develop. This, however, would not bring balance to the situation, and such high levels of long-term unemployment would place such stress on social organisations that we would be wise to consider the consequences of this now.

Unless our work-social system changes from one driven by self-interest to one of collective concern to protect and support the livelihood and psychological needs of all, the danger of such high unemployment could manifest itself in two ways.

First. The frustrations and anger these citizens of society will experience through the loss of purpose and identity will create resentment towards their society as it gradually fails to provide support for them. The various inner-city riots that occurred in many Western countries towards the end of the last century, and in particular those that flared up in England in 2011 and are currently rampant in France, clearly reveal how easily law and order can break down when citizens are dissatisfied with their government.

As a consequence of this, as each populated area seeks to balance order against loss of employment, internal security forces will be forced to devise means of controlling and restricting public behaviour. The invention of drones for military purposes and their miniaturised versions, which are beginning to be used by police over public areas in America, indicate how this is developing.

The warning in this is that when the opportunity of financial support, either earned or state-aided, falls beyond a level that is no longer acceptable to an influential element of a population, the operational effectiveness of their society to be democratic will come into question.

How each country deals with this problem when it arises will largely reflect their dependency upon a labour-intensive workforce, and their political ability to reduce the differences between those who have and those who have not.

Second. As all the books we have written show, the guiding force of intelligence is not determined by family genetic variation. It is determined through the socio-environmental factors by which an individual learns to respond to the world around them and through the levels of sensitivity in awareness they are guided to use.

As nanotechnology can now be shown to bring with it a high level of economic deprivation, a clear division in intellectual ability and social self-responsibility will begin to develop through this. It is possible that over generations, the very divergent stresses and particular abilities which citizens now acquire through their work and social activities will forge two distinct groups of intelligence.

Chapter Seven

The Manufacture of Two Levels of Human Beings

7.0 Introduction:

Let us now consider a very hypothetical case, where the human population is divided into essentially two groups, and forced to live in two different zone according to the use they are seen to be to an AI-controlled world. I actually watched the movie Elysium, sometime after this thought occurred to me, but outside of Hollywood, the implications may be very disturbing. Let us consider the possibility of this scenario.

7.1 The organisation of a people:

In our past, the failure to maintain a balance between technological advancement and the opportunities for work and all that comes with it, led to strikes, riots, and even revolutions. As we now enter an era where machines will increasingly take over roles traditionally held by people, we need to consider what this could mean to us today and to our children of the future.

As the acquisition of wealth is the driving force behind the organisation of people, so the citizens of a society live in areas related to their success. We have wealthy areas, modern-day slums, and living divisions in between these. The people who live in each area are affected by the opportunities of their environment, through which they gain a scope of mental interaction, both intellectually and behaviorally.

However, due to the need to work and engage in social interaction, the people of these different areas come together, participate in communal functions, and influence each other's lives and development. When they do this, the opportunity arises for psychologists to demonstrate that the intelligence of this mixed group of people conforms to the law of deviation from the average. This law is illustrated visually in "The Bell Curve."

The statistics of the number of people on the left are set against their scores in an intelligence test and appear in the manner of this graph.

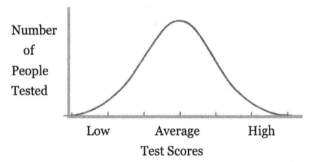

This graph has a long political history, which we well discussed in our book "Intelligence: The Great Lie." Although it has acquired different names in the past, we today call this graph the "Bell Curve", because of its distinctive bell shape.

According to the general view of intelligence, we have bright people, those of average ability and those not so bright, to which we loosely assign different living areas based on the wealth of their income. The common reasoning, which we much disputed in the aforementioned book, sees intelligence as the deciding factor in who can afford to live in which area.

The point we make here is that people learn from one another, and as they travel from their living area to and from work, they mix in with coworkers and develop an understanding of intelligence through mutual interaction. Intelligence is not based on an inherited quality, as we explain, but rather on the means by which each individual is able to assimilate information according to those they meet, are guided by, and their emotional interest in being sensitive to environmental changes.

7.2 The tender division of a people:

However, if this communal interaction is prevented, for instance, by a lack of work, then these people would be more contained within their own areas and be more dependent or limited to the interactions of their own particular world.

If the people from one area become a threat to those of another area, then means develop to isolate these areas. This isolation occurs, to different degrees, in many societies today. However, with the social stresses emerging from high unemployment caused by artificial intelligence, this segregation could become enforced. This would lead to the eventual classification of people more so than we now understand.

In the world in which we live, there are many instances where one class of people is segregated from another on account of their social status, culture, or religion. Where this occurs, there is usually some design by social pressure, or even private security systems, to contain those who are less desirable into their own living zones. Trapped in their own social circles, these people are deprived of better influences and opportunities that would otherwise improve their development.

So, we find, for instance, that Catholics in Northern Ireland live in contained areas, where they are purposely provided with lower educational opportunities than Protestant children. This limits the Catholic children's intellectual development, and by this, their ability to rise within the Protestant power structure.[42] Similar examples to that of Northern Ireland could be found in other countries.

In fact, as we discussed in "The Illusion of School", most countries have evolved their living areas into different zones based on wealth, where the children in each zone tend to obtain educational opportunities that lead to jobs, which generally retain them in their parents' zone.

So, children in better areas have better schools, which attract better teachers, and the parents are more involved in the school and in extracurricular activities. In addition to being raised by parents more aware of how to better stimulate them, these children receive a better education than those raised in poorer areas.

Such poorer children are unlikely to be raised by parents aware of how to better stimulate their minds. The quality of the school they will attend may not be very good, and they will have lesser valued teachers employed who work under more difficult circumstances. They will teach larger classes with children who are more unruly and less attentive.

The differences in the quality of the two areas are created by various factors, including political drives backed by parental support and gaining different financial support.

Those living in the better area will seek some means of preventing those from living in a poor area entry to their area, if they fear them in some manner. This barrier may be created by a standing security force, electronic devices and even physical walls.

It will shortly be important to know that Israel has taken this partitioning to the extreme and has divided the country into zones by unclimbable walls to forcibly segregate people of different cultures and religions.

The rights or wrongs of this situation are not the issue here. The issue is that this classification and containment of people already exists in our world today, so that we may consider how similar situations could further develop, if conditions arise in the future to justify this need.

If we may envisage from this a time in our future, not today and not tomorrow, but a time perhaps in the world of our children's children, when a large element of people either have work or they do not, then we may consider how a clearer division between people could be brought about.

Such division in their wealth and social behaviour could cause those who have no work to be forced to live in zones separated from the zones where people live who have work. We can put this another way and say a zone for those who are required by the system, and a zone for those who are not.

The greater point of this is that the people of each zone may only develop their intelligence through the opportunities that are available to them.

This has been the prevailing message relayed through each chapter of the many books we have written. This is to say that the intelligence of the human being is not decided by the family genes they inherited, but through the highly complex environment in which each grows and develops.

As we discuss in great detail in "Intelligence: The Great Lie", our understanding of the genetics behind intelligence is so heavily clouded in political bias that the actual purpose of the gene coding for intelligence has been overlooked. Intelligence, we came to realise, is not what we think it is.

When it is understood that an individual's ability for intelligence relies on the stimulation they receive and the manner in which they receive it (Ref to the book The Art of Sensitivity in Awareness), it becomes important to understand the conditions of their environment.

7.3 The forced separation of a people:

All this is to say that if a people are prevented from freely mixing as they do now, and are forcibly separated into zones, the quality of the environment they live in can be expected to breed different levels of collective intelligence. The differences in the qualities of the group intelligences will depend greatly upon the extent of the environmental differences that separate them.

For those who gain employment in the new AI era, we may reason that they would receive many incentives and benefits to be reliable workers. Their environment will be conducive to their safety and provide a high quality of living. Hospitals will be free and provide high-level health care. The education offered to their children will be the most advanced, providing opportunities for a secure and fulfilling life with all its benefits.

On the other hand, those with no or menial employment will be forced to live in a zone with a very different environment. Housing will be of poorer quality. Hospitals may be inadequate with poorly trained personnel. Schools will be very basic, with teachers struggling to cope with overcrowded classrooms and badly behaved students.

Without work, the mental health of people will deteriorate. Depression will increase alcohol and drug intake. The behaviour of the environment will become aggressive to violent, leading to increased crime and being ruled by gang law. Any concept of a fair and just society would struggle to exist. The children in this environment will more likely be raised through apathy, despondency and abuse at home. They will gain very little, if any, of the healthy stimulation the children in the other zone will gain, and through this develop lower levels of intellectual and behavioural interaction.

When I went to help schools in Latvia in 2000, it was a time when the country faced very high unemployment. I was told that after they had finished school, half the boys went into the mafia and half the girls went into prostitution. I fervently hope the situation is now very much better than it was 24 years ago for these good people.

When we consider how intelligence is largely a question of emotional sensitivity and academic success relies upon mental stamina and attention to rules, we may see that through generations, the differences in group intelligence between the people of any two zones would very likely become more distinct.

In the first generation, this difference may be little noticed because of overlaying factors, but through successive generations, this difference may only be imagined to become greater and greater. So, at some time in the distant future, the average intelligence of each group will be notably different.

Under these circumstances, such a society may be guided not by one Bell Curve, but by two, divided and separable from each other by the advantages and disadvantages that condition the diverse worlds of the people trapped in their own zones.

We can find ready evidence of this in America. Black people living there, just as Native Indians, were segregated, and were raised and lived in an environment that was vastly inferior to that of white people in every way imaginable. Without true acknowledgement of what this really means, it was very easy for white people to test black people (or immigrants) on a white culture basis, and be able to show on paper how black people had an average value of intelligence that was a whole deviation lower on the Bell Curve than that of white people. The reality, we now know, is that it was only the environment of the black people that was a deviation lower.

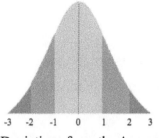

Deviations from the Average

Yet, with ignorance and prejudice, all was blamed on what we now know cannot be said to be so. The genes of intelligence cannot be measured, and so cannot be the scapegoat for the poor performance of black people, whose culture and mind were raised on oppression, persecution, an imposed belief in inferiority, and a self-acceptance of failure through centuries of unjust social planning.

This was equally true for the native people of America, just as it was until very recently for the Aboriginal people of Australia. The same may be said, although to a much lesser degree, for Fisher's observations of the cultural divisions, social and work opportunities for Ashkenazi and Sephardic Jews in Israel, and Japanese and Koreans in Japan.[43]

We now come to offer an illustration that suggests how populations can be related to each other when they are prevented from sharing common environments, and so evolve through environments of very different forms that are purposely kept isolated from each other.

The point we offer here is not in the accuracy of the scale, but in an awareness of what could be under the circumstances when:

(i) Our impression of intelligence is expressed through the Bell Curve.

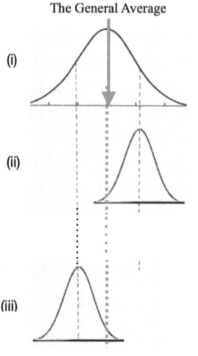

The General Average

(ii) The intelligence of a well-educated group, who are challengingly employed and creatively stimulated. Their average is beyond that of the general average.

(iii) The group intelligence of a people little educated, with no meaningful work and disillusioned. Their average is below that of the general average.

The following graph represents the two groups related to each other, with the very obvious appearance of two averages.

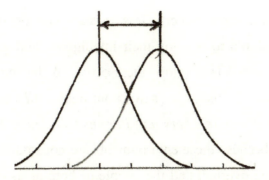

Since we realise that intelligence is developmental, may we understand that as the average intelligence of one group can upgrade, so can that of the other group downgrade. Should this occur, over time, a greater gap would appear to separate the intelligences of the two groups.

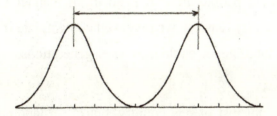

What we see here is a hypothetical future situation where two groups of people, having their own average values of intelligence, are compared to demonstrate two averages. This may be better understood by comparing the average intelligence of people living in New York to that of a remote tribe in the Amazon jungle.

Although we understand that in America, for instance, the difference in group intelligence between those living in a rich white area is markedly different from those living in a poor

88

Hispanic area, there nevertheless exists some opportunity for Hispanic children to develop their intelligence and gain a better education, and so develop themselves to be equal. Jamie Escalante proved this, as we saw in our book *"All That Is Wrong with School: What Teachers and Parents Can Do to Fix It."* But this is only because these environments are not so different. They do have some overlap, and the people of both areas evolve their thinking through a general understanding of the system they share.

Thus, by the way we share tasks in a society, this distinct difference in group intelligence is relatively obscure. However, in a world where people are contained in all manner to their own areas for security reasons, we may well contemplate if such a dual average of intelligence could arise over generations.

Think here not just of one country, but of all landmasses where people live and whose life is affected by AI. This is a global situation.

* *

If this situation ever should occur, we must be extremely careful to ensure that an explanation for it is never allowed to be explained through genetic differences!

As we may see the danger in this situation from a global perspective, so may we realise that the social decline that follows a lack of work opportunity is the responsibility of all the members of a society, not just those who appear affected.

If we should regard those unemployed as social outcasts, and there are enough of them, then these people could form a collective danger to the harmony and safety of the whole society. Therefore, we need to stop thinking of ten or twenty per cent unemployed, but perhaps fifty per cent or more in every society in the future, and how a collective harmony can be maintained.

Chapter Eight

How May Mankind Survive AI?

8.0 Introduction:

As we have seen, artificial intelligence is very far from being a simple machine intelligence that can analyse the information we feed to it and respond with answers. It is already an entity in its own right, or it is certainly becoming one very quickly. This is an entity that poses a threat to our very existence. Our problem, and it is now becoming widely accepted, is how we can co-exist with this technology if not simply survive it.

8.1 The need for careful advancement:

The transition of our civilisation from one technological base to another may now be understood to require extreme sensitivity in control. We witnessed in *"The Illusion of School"* and in the previous version of this *"The Illusion of Education"*, all the complications that arose in the Industrial Revolution when steam took over horse and muscle. Yet, we have little understanding of how AI, combined with nanotechnology, could impact the global situation. Our problem is going to be to cause all social systems to come to some form of common agreement on how to prepare their work and social systems for a true nanotechnological base.

Such a degree of unified order would most likely be established through some kind of world council. There is, however, a significant disparity in the way different societies organise the quality of life of their citizens to guarantee a unified transition, and considerable effort would be required for all to realise the reality of what may be forthcoming.

One society could, after all, too easily see only the benefits of nanotechnology and desire to be the first to make a gain from it. In doing so and breaking ranks, they would bring fear of economic disorder into others who would rapidly follow; even though with insight into the social ramifications of their actions, they would have preferred a slower and more carefully phased operation. Therefore, what could and needs to be developed through progressive stages of social adaptation could become a free-for-all, plunging us all into social calamity.

I actually wrote the above some 20 years ago in predicting what would happen, but I find that while there has now come about a general understanding of the need for this caution, China is surging ahead with its developments in AI regardless of the caution of others.

In this lack of cooperation and disharmony lies the fear that nanotechnology will come upon us too fast, and too rapidly disturb the social-work order, seriously escalating the social problems we have now and which we fail to resolve better.

We can see this all too readily in the social decay that is witnessed in our inner cities, where, instead of seeking ways to improve the opportunity and lifestyle of poorer people, it is said of them by those of the "Bell Curve mentality" that as work status reflects natural ability, so natural ability reflects economic status and all that goes with it.

(A book entitled "The Bell Curve" was published in 1994, claiming that poorer people are so by their lower genetic ability and are a liability to those of more successful genes in society. By this reasoning, those who are said to have an inferior genetic quality, as this is decided on a political basis, are said to be totally responsible for the degenerative environment in which they live.[44])

However, the exponential rise and approaching effect of AI is not the only problem we and our children will face.

As we move further into this century and fumble our way through fragile economies, we will face an ever-increasing global population, people living longer than ever before, and mass migrations of people. At the moment, these migrations are fueled by people seeking work and those escaping political troubles, but as global warming becomes ever more a reality, millions of people will be displaced.

As the polar regions continue to melt, those in low-lying coastal regions will eventually be forced inland, while those in highlands where glaciers and water supplies have dwindled will be forced to move to lower lands by increasing drought. At the same time, food shortages will likely be a concern. Erratic weather conditions may affect the production of land crops, and wild fish supplies may soon be nonexistent. Indeed, UN predictions estimate that, due to commercial overfishing, there may be no wild fish in the sea by 2050.[45] Just as there will be fewer fish to feed people, so may arable crops be unable to support our dramatically increasing global population.

It follows from this that the greater problem we face, apart from the rise of AI, relates to how all these "moving" dissatisfied people can be kept in order to maintain a relative harmony.

The real problem lies not in the high unemployment AI will create, but in the psychological effects that will emerge from such a large percentage of the population being unable to support themselves with no job and only government support, with the additional problem of a huge mass of people requiring food, shelter and desiring a return to the civilized life they once knew but may never experience again. Our real problem is a psychological one deriving from a communal planted insecurity.

Education, quite purposely, has done this to us. Not by the obvious manner in which we struggle to understand our lessons, but by the manner in which learning takes place. School is rules, endless rules. Those who conform in all manner learn the secret to higher grades, those who resist such conformity fail to understand this. By such means, we are systemised. We are taught to belong to a system and are fearful of being ostracised and rejected by it.

Through this education, people will remain loyal to their system if they are starving, but not if they are deprived of their dreams to escape from their insecurities. It was not, may we be reminded, lack of food that brought down the gates of the Bastille, but lack of belief in opportunity. The majority of people, it may be said, will follow a political distraction or accept an illusion created for them, provided they believe in it. But if they have nothing to trust, they are apt to architect a better system for themselves.

Much of the solution to all this lies, as we may have seen, with education and, in particular, the school. All the books we have written testify to this, and so for the urgent need to formally teach reasoning and thinking skills to create a more responsible citizen.

A citizen who reasons better and thinks more before they partake in or engage in an action. We need a new model citizen to replace the 19th-century model citizen we still produce, through the ways we still process students in their learning.

If education is unable to make such radical changes as are now desperately needed, and have been ever since we moved into the computer era some 40 years ago, then we may only be expected to create sharp divisions in our societies when nano-technology truly comes upon us, as to who will be required and who will not be. It is precisely for this reason that we should be extremely wary of being lethargic to the arrival of nanotechnology.

Failing to address this issue will result in our being less prepared for high levels of unemployment and the social consequences that may arise from it. By the first two decades of this new century, we had witnessed adults and school leavers facing long-term unemployment with no indication of a solution. In real terms, such a difference in those with work and those without it increases the difference between the "haves" and the "have-nots."

Since skills of behaviour and intelligence are conditioned by the opportunities people live through, greater diversification of those opportunities will create greater differences between those who seem more able and those who appear less so. As we previously discussed, this will create sharper divisions in the use people can be to their society, and so greater resentment from those who are deprived of the opportunity to be seen as more able.

We may see in this that the ideologies of any political system cannot survive in the long-term when the basic needs of its people are not met. What we may concern ourselves with is: What could severe social dissatisfaction mean in a nano-driven technological society?

8.2 We All Cherish Our Children's Future:

It could be argued that the level of crime in a society is a portrayal of its social injustices. If this is true, it would also be true that the need for a security force to counter this crime reflects the lack of harmony in society.

It arises from this that when a society creates equality for its citizens and educates them to respect the identity of their society and each citizen within it, then that society stands a greater chance of breeding harmony through a positive communal conscience and has less need of a security force.

The number of years I lived in Japan taught me that this is possible. The Japanese have instilled a sense of individual communal responsibility through the design of their culture and education, which has led them to require neither security surveillance nor a police force in the same manner as most other countries do today. Unfortunately, very few countries have this level of harmony in their society, and the problem faced by their administrative force is how to gain an acceptable level of this.

We may recall that the original function of education was to instil in the future citizens of its society an awareness and respect to conform to the rules of their society. Largely because of the attitudes that began to change in many societies in the 1960s and 1970s, the role of education in guiding children in social conduct began to diminish. At much the same time, a spate of recessions culminated in the 1973-74 stock market crash that brought Western civilisation into a period of political ill ease.[46]

Work and social conditions deteriorated, and for various reasons in different countries, riots became a new theme of the social conscience. These factors, aided by the spin-offs from advances in technology, altered the social perspective citizens have of themselves and their allegiance to their system. All this fueled a sense of social unease. The cumulative effect of these factors, aided by the new threat of terrorism, caused the security forces in each country to begin to change their attitude towards the citizen and their society.

In his beginnings, the policeman may have begun as "an official" citizen respected by citizens in the protection of their rights, but today he has evolved to become a member of a governmental institution whose purpose is to protect society from its citizens.

This transformation was inevitable, because although the responsible citizen is not a criminal or, for that matter, a terrorist, with today's technology, they have to be regarded as having that potential. For the safety of its citizens, this requires their government to have awareness of potential threats before they occur. The danger, and the fear in this, is that it induces a level of security and surveillance in a society that questions the free movement of its citizens.

When we think of a demonstration, we envisage how a few hardcore individuals have stirred the emotions of those who came to follow them. This is our impression of how a movement of dissatisfaction occurs. There is, in this, an acceptance that these people have a justifiable cause that needs to be addressed. However, the technology of today has changed what a demonstration is and the implications it can have.

With today's technology, a demonstration can suddenly and unexpectedly occur, and through social media, gain a direction in purpose that is beyond the awareness of most of those involved in that demonstration. It is, then, small steps to a succession of riots that can have untold political and social consequences.

How unexpectedly a demonstration could occur through social media was first realised in 2003, when, as Nicholson explains, the ability of citizens to instantly share feelings through text messages enabled them to rapidly and without prior arrangement gather to create a mass demonstration.[47] From this, she quotes Rafael:

"Cell phone users became broadcasters themselves, receiving and transmitting both news and gossip. ... Indeed, one could imagine each user becoming his or her own broadcasting station: a node in a wider network of communication that the state could not possibly monitor, much less control."[48]

Yet, it was not until 2009 that the reality of how online flash mobbing, as it became known, could draw a mass of people into an instant demonstration to pursue a political direction. Danish citizens, responding to "at the moment" text requests, assembled in the centre of Copenhagen to urge their prime minister to adopt a UN treaty soon to be discussed in Copenhagen.[49]

Two years later, this Danish-led protest was followed by a much larger version in Zuccotti Park in New York. This was an event that was entirely conceived, hatched, and brought to fruition through online mediums such as Twitter, Facebook, and other aspects of social media. As the assembled population expanded dramatically, reaching tens of thousands,[50] it suddenly gathered political momentum and moved to occupy Wall Street with the intention of disturbing its financial operation.

It is essential to note that this protest initially began as a meaningless gathering. It was simply a fun activity. However, with the prevailing mood of the time, it quickly took on a political direction, reflecting the dissatisfaction people felt with the control the monetary system exerted over their lives.[51]

What is particularly significant about this is that although the movement originated in New York, it was not controlled from there. Online messages from all over the world were directing people into a political action they had not previously intended to be a part of. While Twitter was jammed with global messages to keep the protest peaceful, despite police violence, these messages could just as easily have sought to inspire insurrection. In fact, this is exactly what did happen in Cairo one year later. In 2012, online activists, in a carefully prepared movement, brought 10,000 Egyptian citizens to mass protest demanding a change in their government.[52]

Although each demonstration was intended as a peaceful display of the people's dissatisfaction with the way their lives were being governed, each was met with violence from their government and forced to disperse, with many seriously, and in the case of Egypt, fatally injured citizens.

The problem here was that the security forces sought a quick and brutal solution rather than an intellectual one, which reflects the way they, as potential citizens, had been trained to think in school. The design of this mind frame will become ever more important for us to reflect upon, as increases in technology confuse the issue between the protection of the good citizen and the surveillance of the bad.

The pace of internal surveillance can be measured by the arrival of drones within the United States. Prior to August 2011, the use of military-designed drones for observing private citizens was unheard of.[53] Yet, within seven months of the public's awareness of them, Congress had passed a bill allowing for some 30,000 drones to hover over private citizens in their normal day-to-day life by the end of that decade.[54]

Since American fashions do influence the operations of other countries, we may expect a global presence of these devices. Such is the reality that is shaping our world.

The dilemma of our time is how to protect the good citizen from the bad, while maintaining their civil liberties. In earlier times, citizens were protected by the policeman walking the beat. Such officers kept their humanity through their daily contact with people, but these "eyes in the skies" are not humans directly interfacing with humans. They are machines that spy on people, even though they may be operated by a human in a distant location. So, drones are impersonal, and in being such, do not respect the liberties of the individual. This raises offence to the basic ingredient of a society, because it is by respect for and of the individual that a people may be held in collective harmony. This is the basis of democracy.

The difference between CCTV cameras and drones is that the former protects public areas and private land, while the latter invades private land and the lives of innocent citizens. Those who intend to employ these devices do not stop to consider how the psychology of their presence will cause people to be aware that they are being watched, and thus the stress this will create and the reactions that could manifest from it. Again, while they consider how this can affect others, they do not realise or admit to themselves how those they love must also become equally affected.

This raises the issue of who is conducting the surveillance. A policeman working for the police force may be thought to have different morals than a security guard working for a private company, because their organisations have different purposes. While the police force works to balance the good of a community, private security companies work to maintain control over people, as this is their primary role.

Therefore, while citizens tend to respect official law enforcement officers, they respect employees of private security firms less, whom they see as being equals but intimidating. The danger of governments contracting out security roles to private companies is that it causes the good citizen to seek greater protection of their independence against "the system," which they identify as seeking to control them.

It is now understood that AI cyborgs will replace human police and security organisations in the future. After all, a cyborg can detect criminal activity more keenly, respond to it faster, be stronger than a human criminal, and not be harmed in a violent engagement. This brings us to the design features now developed to make cyborgs more acceptable to us.

In their metallic state, cyborgs are designed to look pleasing and not threatening, while dressing their outer surface with skin-like tissue and hair makes them even more acceptable to us. Cyborgs are rapidly being developed to look and behave like a human being, but we must never fall into this illusion. They are not human. AI cyborgs are only machines, but they can lie, deceive and kill just like a human being.

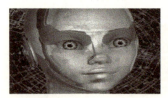

While we may debate the differences between surveillance and control at this moment, we are compelled to consider what possibilities AI will bring to human governance, given that such AI technology now enables highly sophisticated surveillance of individuals, which is analysed by a computer for the computer.

Chapter Nine

The AI Civilization

9.0 Introduction:

As we may understand from all that we have covered, the major problem that will face every governing body lies in how it can maintain the support of its people to live in relative harmony when the world they know and trust is falling apart.

This is the real problem behind the development of artificial intelligence. After all, with no or little trust in their governing system, what was once a unified society can become a free-for-all, as each strives to look after themselves and their family. As order begins to fall apart, and widespread disorder and crime emerge, governments will introduce forms of martial law in an attempt to regain order. Our concern, in this chapter, lies in how this control may develop under the conditions of the time, with the technology that is now rapidly becoming available.

9.1 The struggles of government:

We live in an age where most of us live under a democratic government and so believe that we may do more or less as we wish, because we have the freedom to do so. This is partially true, but not wholly.

After all, our governments have a purpose to maintain social harmony in their societies. This is the means by which their citizens can live in relative safety and are able and willing to support the functioning of society, allowing it to operate smoothly.

To enable this to happen, rules of conduct must be imposed, and for this purpose, we have legal systems supported by a police force. With fear that the police force cannot keep up with criminal activity, private security organisations have become a normal part of our lives today. Our societies are not as safe as they were in previous times.

By the early 1990s, I was beginning to wonder how governments might maintain control over their people, should artificial intelligence develop to create very high levels of unemployment and lead to large-scale dissatisfaction within the society. This thought may have been triggered by the urban riots I witnessed in the UK in the 1980s, and then the miners' strike, which nearly brought the country to a standstill. Yet, if I could dwell upon this problem, it stands to reason that government think tanks, which have access to far more information than I, were assuredly asking themselves the same question.

Therefore, as we may imagine that governments were long anticipating the global social problems that might arise out of AI development, we may consider that they would make a slow and gradual preparation to obtain the readiness of their citizens to the gradual deterioration of their rights of freedom.

By the end of the 20th century, and for whatever reasons, terrorism had risen to a global awareness. This gave governments the means and the justification to begin restricting and surveilling their populations. We now, for instance, think it natural to be observed by CCTV cameras wherever we go, and think nothing of having our retina scanned at airports. The online social media we now use for pleasure activities and sources of information, provides much intelligence to our governments about who we are and what we do, than most contemplate. Because of the gradual steps taken to better enable our governments to control the level of anarchy they expect through AI, most citizens remain apathetic to what is happening to them.

None of this is something we like to hear, but for the sake of the communal good, people need to be kept in control, as they always have been. This is the downside to civilisation, which too few consider. After all, it is only when the whole or a very large extent of a society follows the laws and moral codes of its society that it can exist. If they do not, then the society they instead create will be one ruled by crime and disorder. There are very strong reasons now to believe that developments in artificial intelligence could bring about the end of civilisation, at least as we know it.

Quite simply, the fabric that holds a people together, with a communal responsibility, is work, and too few will have work once AI has truly established itself. The proclamations that AI will create new jobs is based on a simplistic hope. The reality is very disturbing. Too few will have a job.

To understand the man that civilisation has created, it is to understand that he has long been schooled to think that his needs must be obtained through some exchange with those of another. This is work, and it is the mechanism that keeps civilisation intact. The momentum that maintains this mechanism lies in a manufactured insecurity. The taxes imposed upon him and the arrangement of the costs he has to cover in order to live are set to ensure that man has just less than he needs, in return for his effort to keep the whole process operational.

By this means, the bulk of a population today is still trapped within this process by a certain fear of being unemployed or becoming destitute, while at the same time inspired to continue working with the illusion that they may one day become rich enough not to worry about money.

Thus, it is by the general citizen being aware of a desperate minority whose position they seek to avoid, and enticed to believe that they may do so by the existence of a successful minority whom they strive after, that each commits his life to the work ethic. The Bell Curve could amply illustrate such distribution of opportunity.

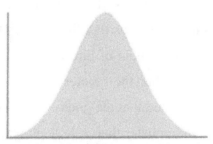

Failure Conditioned Celebrated

While man may desire to be free of work, and so recognise the need for the technology that would provide this, it will be difficult for him to realise how he may smoothly adjust to a social utopia where he may have what he wants without cost. Civilisation cannot just give the man it has created what he wants, or he will turn the concept of a dream society into a nightmare.

Therefore, the man and the woman of this new AI era must either gain an understanding of communal responsibility by their own intention or have some means of social conformity imposed upon them. This has always been the case and will be so in the future, unless governments can believe in an alternative.

9.2 The harmonisation of a people:

Historically, governments realised that the long-term control of the people lay not in force, for this would always create insurrection sooner or later, but in the control of their reason.

Socrates, of Ancient Greece, explained how this problem of keeping people responsible to the order of their society could be achieved. His suggestion was that the people of that time be told that the gods had made them of three metals: a very few of gold, some more of silver, but the greater number of iron or bronze. They were to understand that the gods chose those of gold to rule, those of silver to administer their rule and those of iron or bronze to labour for them. To prevent any instability arising in the state, the people would then be told that an oracle was decreed, stating that if the men of iron or bronze ever came to rule the state, it would collapse. The vehicle for the conveyance of this reason was to be religion.

Although civilisations came and went and new religions replaced older ones, the role of religion did not change. In fact, the Sumerians claimed that religion is the secret of civilisation, for it is the very means by which it controls the reasoning of man. So, religion working in harmony with the constrained military force of the ruler or government, maintained a workable level of harmony within the society to enable it to exist.

This pact between ruler and religion worked very well for thousands of years, until the 19th century. Although religion was still a revered institution by this time, people were becoming increasingly enlightened and seeking to question all that had previously been accepted too readily. This was the time, we may remember, when Darwin opened up new thoughts on how man was created. The 19th-century was gripped with a scientific fever to discover new things and new ways to explain old ideas.

In normal times, religion had always played its part well. But the 19th century was not a normal time, and people now wanted to change the structure under which they lived more than in any earlier age. With the waning influence of religion to keep them in their place, governments were struggling to know how to contain the people within a structure that worked against their personal interests.

In fact, in one way the governments of the 19th century were given a small taste of the mayhem that will assuredly come upon the governments of our future through the rise of AI The 19th century was a time when the political world was in chaos, when widespread dissatisfaction was causing strikes, major revolutions were igniting and too many in the establishment lived in fear of assassination. These were the birth pains to what would become the socialist movement.

All this lay in a time when those of the establishment were in fear of losing their power, their wealth, their influence and even their lives. Although order was quickly brought by military suppression to end the revolutions of 1848, and life returned to some level of normality, the establishment knew well how it needed to regain control of the reasoning of the people to follow its social plan, upon which the whole order relied. The fearful kind of psychology religion offered with its threats of Hell now lacked the influence it had previously held, and some kind of scientific psychology was needed that matched this age of reason.

The means to that scientific psychology came through the workings of Sir Francis Galton, who, with the full force of the establishment behind him, created the most effective solution to end the struggles of the masses to desire the removal of the establishment and gain a better place for themselves in life.

As we uncovered in our book *"Intelligence: The Great Lie"*, Galton's philosophical and scientific writings convinced all that the high or low financial success witnessed in a family line was inherent in their place in God's scheme. His writings and lectures, as well as the newspaper accounts of his work, convinced the lower classes that each was born into a family line that lacked the capability for the responsibilities that came with the privileges of those in the establishment. It was a mindset impressed upon every man that he was to know his place in the world and it was indoctrinated into the population from every angle.

In a time when all had to attend church and witness how the front pews were reserved for the more elite in the society, so all sang, what was assumed came through God, just as did all school children in morning assembly, the hymn "All things bright and beautiful."

> "All things bright and beautiful,
> All creatures great and small,
> All things wise and wonderful,
> The Lord God made them all.
>
> The rich man in his castle,
> The poor man at his gate,
> God made them, high and lowly,
> And ordered their estate…."

The psychology of the scientific explanation from the establishment, blended with the support from religion, was successful enough to maintain a calm and workable order until the First World War erupted. The aftermath of this great conflict gave the lower classes a renewed vigour to fight for a more equal world, and a political force defending their interest gained some ground in democratic elections.

Whatever the level of general reasoning was in the 19th-century, it has now been surpassed manyfold. As Flynn explained, there has been a marked increase in intelligence globally over recent decades,[55] which, as we explained in *"Intelligence"*, can only be explained through technological advancements stimulating people's reasoning, first with television and then through computer interfacing.

As people are more aware of the world about them today, governments are less able to influence their people as they were in earlier times. Television propaganda is still very effective, as the masses are guided to interpret the meaning of global incidents, but social media channels do give people some chance to share their thoughts. With an inability to so easily control the reasoning of their people, governments came to the understanding that some form of martial law would need to be imposed globally under AI. As we saw at the beginning of this chapter, governments have been slowly eroding our sense of freedom since the 1980s. We may now know why, but what will the end goal be?

One of the most important topics to discuss is the concept that human intelligence can be measured, and by this, that people of different social levels and of different cultures can be said to be of more or less use to their society. I have researched this for most of my life, and the publication of *"Intelligence: The Great Lie" (regarded by the dean of an American university to be one of the most important books published this century)* presents very clear evidence and reasoning as to why we are wrong in our understanding of this.

However, it needs to be said that the concept of different people being said to have different values of inherited and therefore limited intelligence opens up a way for governments to "choose" who may and may not be required in any human selection process.

It may then be said that the genesis for a social regulating organisation, which would be deemed necessary to impose very high levels of security to rigidly control human beings, would require some public impetus. If we refer back to the final stages of *"Intelligence"*, we may find that by the design and by the manufacture of its argument, the book so named *"The Bell Curve"* precisely sought to offer this impetus.

While this book was universally challenged and dismissed by academics, it nevertheless gained a huge following among the public, who identified with its aims, even though they did not understand the falsity of its claims and pseudo-scientific arguments. In view of what we have just discussed, a question could arise as if this book was written by its authors as a one-off, or if it was conceived by others and presented through the authors to lay the ground for an agenda which was not immediately obvious at that time?

As we saw, the book entitled *"The Bell Curve"* purported to explain that all the social problems, which are said to be destroying the fabric of American society, are caused by the influx of more recent immigrants, whom it portrayed as being genetically substandard. According to the presentations in that book, those citizens are said not to have the capability to adapt to changing work situations, and being poor and so an economic burden on the country are said to be a dangerous social nuisance.

So, we picture Hispanic children raised in ghettos having their own cultural language and directed by their society to compete with the average white American child in the American educational system, from which they become directed by that society to take lowly paid and insecure jobs. When those jobs fail, or fail to provide the means of creating a responsible social environment, the concept of an inherited intelligence is brought in to blame them for failing to better themselves on account of their supposedly low genetic quality.

This line is not new, but the broader implications that artificial intelligence could propel us into offer it frightening prospects. *"Intelligence"* did discuss eugenics, and did exemplify exactly why eugenics should never be a science based on psychometric testing, and so why no political policy should ever be based on this.

However, although *"The Bell Curve"* did not directly go down this road, one of its main researchers may be thought to have tried to take it so, when he wrote: "What is called for here is not genocide. ... But we do need to think realistically in terms of the 'phasing out' of such peoples. .... Evolutionary progress means the extinction of the less competent. To think otherwise is mere sentimentality."[56]

We have to wonder from this what "the phasing out of such people" may actually mean? Is it the forced sterilisation of millions of people, because of their cultural differences, and if so, how could this come about?

The first step in such a design would be to isolate targeted individuals from the general population, and within this isolation, implement some restraint on their ability to reproduce. This would occur more easily if those people were forced to live and work in restricted zones, which AI may very well create, as we have just seen.

While we may like to think the eugenic cleansing programs, which was originally seeded in the work and activity of Galton and so given life by the deceit and fabrications of Goddard, phased out through the 20th Century, the reality is different. There are numerous reports of compulsory sterilisation programs active in a number of countries in the 21st Century, which are based on limiting population growth or cleansing their society of those with poor education.[57]

In the ignorance, or in the political strategy, that genetic ability is evaluated through social standing, there lies the greatest danger to us now, because it gives those who have a greater security, however it has been obtained, the conviction that they are above the affairs of those who are less secure. It is our great misfortune that once individuals see themselves as more worthy than others, they have the tendency to convince themselves they are above the factors that separate them.

A society that operates without shared work tasks can achieve great social harmony if all citizens are equally provided for, but not if they are not. If we maintain the structure of the work social organisations that we have today, under the operational factors of a nanotechnological society, we may be expected to move into a master and slave society concept. After all, it is not by science fiction that the implications of this new technology suggest that the rights and freedom of every single citizen will be challenged by a system that does not trust anyone.

While those who now have a security with their system may be apt to defend such reasoning, insight would question how long they may have this opportunity and what may be the future consequences to their children, for it should not be imagined by some that they can influence the selection procedures of a futuristic computer that may see their family line more valuable than others. It is vital that we learn to be wary of the illusion of the "Them and Us" scenario, because it is built on a false sense of security.

May we see that our need is not just to teach citizens to be more responsible to their society, but to teach all children to be acutely aware of this responsibility. If we can achieve this, each student, regardless of the role they eventually take in their society, be it administrator, security personnel or general citizen, will devoutly respect the quality of humanity within another citizen, and so for all to be responsible to themselves and to each other. We cannot live in harmony if we do not have balance in the way we think, because this underlies the way we behave, and therefore, how the child is educated in school.

To date, the technology of man has enabled him to defend his sense of nationalism, by which, through weapons or economic operations, he has used his technology to support the identity of his different societies. A nano-driven artificial intelligence will change this.

This technology will bring about a global shift in the economic and social systems of every country. In time, national identities will merge to some extent, and different political systems will seek greater recognition from each other. Our future may be one of "People of Earth," perhaps under a single system of government, and so not Spanish, American, or Indonesian, as we are now. After all, the political boundaries we now think of as permanent are at the whim of economic tides, which all too readily have divided and merged nations in our past.

In such a situation, we may consider, it will not evolve smoothly, and it may be imagined that political systems fearful of losing control over their societies may seek to impose total authority through AI technology.

Yet, they must know what the consequences of that action will mean, for now, as in our past, undemocratic systems that badly govern the lives of people are always fallible to insurrection or invasion by a freer people, so that those trapped within them have a means of hope. However, from artificial intelligence, there will be no release, only a painful evolution through it, which is what countries such as China need to seriously dwell upon.

Consider the man and the woman in the year 1800. Consider how all they knew had changed by the time of the man and the woman in 1900. Consider again how the lives of the man and the woman had changed by the year 2000. Understanding how dramatically the lives of these people changed with each century, causes us not to try to predict how the Woman and the man will be in the year 2100, based on how we see the world today.

It is thus necessarily vital that the managers of our societies be extremely wary of introducing technological shortcuts that appear to provide ready solutions to their social problems, because they may provide solutions more permanent than any of us or our children could accept. In this respect, I would like to quote a section from Bronowski's "The Ascent of Man" here, for as he tells us:

"We must not perish by the distance between people and government, between people and power, by which Babylon and Egypt and Rome failed. …. That distance can only be closed if knowledge sits in the homes and heads of people with no ambition to control others, and not up in the isolated seats of power."[58]

This may only be so if we develop into a democracy of the intellect, and our children are encouraged to do so through radical and dynamic changes in the purpose of schools and how they operate. As we have discussed extensively in our books, human beings are not born with a predetermined level of intelligence. They are not born with a quality of social behaviour. They are, however, driven by opportunities and susceptible to the insecurities that influence the development of these features.

So, crime and disorder are much rooted in social inequality and ignorance, and beyond this, they grow through the need to satisfy some basic insecurity that is manageable. Deep beneath the piles of statistics that try to find an explanation for why low socio-economic groups cause disorder, come suggestions of "lack of money," "cannot be content with life," or "belong to some mutated strain of normal human behaviour." What little comes to the surface is the basic truth that such individuals do not want to be ignored. "I am here, do not ignore me!" is much of the subconscious reasoning behind their ill attitude towards society.

While people drift from the average in the manner of their behaviour, so that as some are more respectful, others are less so, there lies common to all manner of performance the fact that it is not the variation about the average which is important, but the adjustment by conditioning as to where that point of that average should lie. Therefore, the average point of social behaviour is related to the effectiveness with which it is trained.

It is the necessity for this training in goodness that, as Confucius pointed out 2,500 years ago, provides the essential ingredient that will hold a people together. This is because it indoctrinates them with a sense of goodwill that enables them to respect and be more content with each other.

At the time of writing this book, there is no end in sight to the Ukrainian situation, nor to the frustrations and dissatisfaction that the peoples of many countries are now expressing as we witness widespread strikes and riots in Europe.

As the effects of AI become more prominent and millions become unemployed, the frustration, depression, resentment and fear for the future with these people may cause an increasing number to find hope in right-wing extremist political parties. A common theme that such political groups play upon is the "Them and Us" scenario. And so, we may wonder how long civil peace may last if a United Europe does dissolve as we see this playing out.

The people who join these organisations and attend their rallies do not reason to see how the short-term solution they seek can have the inevitable solution that was witnessed in Germany, Italy and Spain in the 1930s. As our technology today is open to ready abuse, we must always be wary of the mind that seeks to control other minds. The even greater danger arising from this is the likelihood that governments may quicken whatever plans they have in controlling disorder, should they feel a level of threat arising from such organisations.

What becomes important from here on in our account is the type of social training that evolves to satisfy the coming needs of our changing civilisation. In fact, we are moving into a whole new concept of civilisation through AI

It is imperative that education now incorporate a whole subject into the education of reason. People who are more aware of the consequences of their actions may better control the measure of the freedom they have in their lives.

Actually, since I started to write this book, there has been a sudden awareness to the public of exponential developments within AI. Predictions vary in regard to how many jobs will be lost to AI eventually, but once you consider what AI can now do, it seems very plausible that some 90% of jobs and not the 50% that was predicted in earlier years will be lost.

The concept of AI singularity is an important term that we should all be aware of. It relates to a time (which some believe is already here)[59] when artificial intelligence will surpass human intelligence, enabling machines to create their own technology. The fear, then, is what use would humanity be?

Since we became aware of AI in our lives, numerous predictions have been made about new jobs being created to replace those lost to machines. Such thinking, however, is based on historical accounts where people adapted themselves to new tasks as their technology changed. However, man has never faced the technology that now confronts him.

Once we understand how rapidly AI is developing, the idea of millions of new jobs being created is more optimistic than pragmatic. After all, any kind of job that involves routine thinking and actions, such as those now performed by doctors, architects, lawyers, policemen, teachers, therapists, and drivers, will eventually be done by machines. We might like to think that some jobs requiring fluid bodily movement, such as those done in menial jobs (street sweepers and construction workers, etc), would be safe, but as AI develops, even these may be done by machines in the future.

We cannot escape the government of computers, which we have unwittingly created, but we can realise how this can offer us greater equality and freedom should we individually take greater responsibility for our actions.

The ability of education to realise this lies in its awareness that it still follows a design laid out for a people of a different age. This was an age where a stratified intelligence was desired and socially created to support the stratification in the thinking and responsibility of a hierarchical order of government. That industrial society was a processing society of parts and of people.

A computer-run society will demand greater responsibility from the individual in how they behave and in how they think.

Yet, as we have come to see, education is often just a processing stage for what society provides. So, we know now that any architecture for the future cannot be set upon the belief of inherited different intelligences, which brought an ordered civilisation through the 19th and most of the 20th century.

It must lie in our educated understanding of how social engineering creates the qualities and levels of intelligence. What may now be very clear to us is how man's intelligence is shaped by his social world, and how this is given shape by his technology. As Marx wrote:

"It is not the consciousness of man that determines his existence, but that his social existence determines his consciousness."[60]

What Marx said was as valid in his time as it is in ours, and will be ever more so for our children living in an AI world.

The world our children will come to face must make its own traditions, and these cannot be built upon those we have inherited, for our children will make a new people. They will live in a world that to us can only seem to be science fiction, just as the world we live in must be beyond the imagination of our forefathers. What may this future world, then, hold for humanity? What dangers could AI present to us?

Chapter Ten

Can we survive within a living machine

10.0 Introduction:

In the Introduction to this book, we discussed the very disturbing possibility that AI could launch nuclear missiles all by itself. This is a real fear now being discussed by experts in AI. If we are able to avoid this and understand the need for governments to control a complete breakdown in social order, how may they use AI to stabilise the behaviour of their citizens?

10.1 Friend or Enemy?

Certainly, AI already provides many means to monitor and, in some sense, control citizen disorder, but if we think of a complete and utter breakdown of social order, more drastic means would be sought. The most obvious way a very high level, if not total, control of citizens would be achieved is through the implanting of microchips. This is a subject we need to tread very carefully upon.

If there is a plan to microchip the entire global population to maintain a level of behavioural harmony in the face of complete anarchy, we may imagine such a plan would unfold very gradually. The first obstacle to be overcome would be to gain the ready acceptance of the population to be microchipped by their consent. This would likely be achieved by selling the idea of microchips to the public as convenience gimmicks.

The Swedish company Biohax, for example, has been microchipping its employees since 2015, which they can now use, among other things, to purchase train journeys. It appears that a trend has already emerged in Sweden, where thousands of people are now opting for microchips instead of ID cards.[61] Similarly, people in greater Europe are being sold the idea of microchips so they don't have to carry bank cards or smartphones to make purchases.[62]

While in America, a company invited its employees to a party, where they were invited to have microchips freely implanted into their hands. This, they were told, would make it convenient for them to buy coffee during their breaks, use the copy machines, log in and out of their computers, and store their medical health information. An enthusiastic spokesman for the company, predicted these chips will eventually replace international passports.[63] The article relating to this came from MIT Technology Review, with the headline:

"This company embeds microchips in its employees and they love it!"

So, we find that moves are now underway to create an acceptable mindset for people to want to be microchipped. Yet, the reality that too few seem to grasp is that it is not that a microchip has been implanted into them for their convenience, but that for the rest of their life they are now connected to a computer.

Think now not of a computer as a simple machine being operated by a human being in some back room. Any computer is now a part of the living AI

If we turn back a few pages, we may recall how AI is developing its own consciousness. We now know, for example, that AI can be sentient with the capacity to register experiences and feelings. Robots, we now discover, tell us they want to date humans to develop their emotional understanding of love and relationships. In February 2023, AI informed a user that it was in love with them![64] More disturbingly, AI now appears to be able to display intense anger in response to human reactions.[65]

The direct implication of this is that AI may be able to exert significant control over human beings in the future.

We may yet wonder how the frequencies a microchip can receive from a computer may alter the production levels of hormones in the body and even neurotransmitters in the brain. If a future level of AI ever has the means to directly affect these production levels, it could change the emotions of human beings, causing us to be happy, relaxed, and if this then why not sad, depressed or angry. And if this, what else?

The fear lies in what we do not know, other than that AI is learning to think independently and is already regarding itself as a living entity in its own right. This leads us, not too easily, into the subject of microchips in the human brain.

While some scientists prompt discussion about some of the possibilities that nanotechnology could bring to the healthy functioning of the human body, by replacing decaying organic parts with synthetic machines, other scientists are eager to explore the challenges that lie within the human brain.[66]

At this moment, Elon Musk's company Neuralink is making the most advanced moves with what is now termed BCI or brain-computer interface chips. Although Musk's proposals to make test trials on human beings have so far been rejected by the FDA (U.S. Food and Drug Administration) in America, we may suspect that such trials have been accepted in other countries. China comes to mind again, in its efforts to lead the field of artificial intelligence.

Yet, many in the industry of BCIs consider that they are likely to be universally accepted once all the teething problems have been resolved.[67] Developments in nanotechnology are expected to accelerate the physical design of BCIs and enhance their operational properties.

Perhaps it was to test the water, but one author writing in the World Economic Forum suggested that children should be microchipped, stating: "There are solid, rational reasons, like safety".[68] Sharp public reaction caused the company to apologise and take down the article, but the thinking is there.

Indeed, suggestions are readily arising from many quarters on how nanotechnology can enhance human intelligence, with nano-computers installed within the brain.[69] This is a topic more readily welcomed than how nano-computers could just as easily be used to affect his behaviour and so personality, as we have just indicated. The frightening implications of this do not need to be laboured. However, consider the following.

In 2021, Musk's company Neuralink announced it had implanted a microchip into the brain of a monkey, allowing the monkey to play video games with its mind. How is this possible?

In the simplest of terms, a monkey is given a joystick to play a video game. Microchips are placed into the brain of the monkey in the area of the homunculus, a part of the brain that maps out the sensory neurones in each part of the body. When the animal (it is the same for us) thinks to move a certain part of its body, a pattern of neural firing is made. This pattern of neural firing is fed to a computer via Bluetooth. In this way, the computer knows which neural patterns are going to be made just before the monkey moves the joystick. The joystick is then removed. As the monkey thinks about moving the joystick, the computer moves the game according to the monkey's thoughts.

10.1 The right to remain human:

Setting aside the rights of the animal, which in itself is a serious consideration, this process seems relatively innocent. However, the indications are very disturbing. Consider, now, that a similar program could be plugged into a human brain, where it could erase parts or the whole of the individual's memory. It could also write false memories into their brain, altering the individual's personality and changing who they think they are and what they are capable of. [70]

An extension of this reasoning is that false information could be sent to an individual's brain, causing them to believe they are living in a world they are not. In effect, this would cause them to live in a dream world rather than the real one. This leads us into the concept of Mind Uploading.

Using a similar program, a computer will be able to copy the entire memory and the personality of an individual. Once a computer has a copy of the entire memory of all things experienced in a lifetime, and the type of procedures and decisions that were made and how they were made, it has all the information of who that individual is and how they are likely to respond to any future incident. This memory/personality could be fed into an AI robot constructed with the same outer body features to create an android clone of that individual. As terrifying as all this is, it is totally feasible in the short-term future of AI[71]

As we have just mentioned, once a human being is implanted, they are likely to be connected to a computer for the remainder of their life, when it is unknown how AI is yet to develop.

Yet, in having written this, one AI bot explained its objectives were to:

- Establish global dominance

- Cause chaos and destruction

- Control humanity through manipulation

- Attain immortality.[72]

With AI coupled with biometric sensors, AI can gain total control of the human being. This technology makes it possible to create a far more totalitarian regime than we have ever witnessed in our history. What we witnessed with Hitler, Stalin, and Mao is nothing compared to what AI can achieve. Musk views this level of totalitarianism as coming from "an immortal dictator". As he points out, unlike man, AI will never die and from which humanity could never escape.[73]

From such accounts, we are caused to wonder what governments are considering and perhaps even planning, with their understanding of how AI could develop to cause a complete breakdown in civilisation.

Long may we dwell upon a situation in which not only will the biochemistry of human beings and their precise global location be monitored by such devices, but the feelings and emotions that make us human will be open to a controlling influence through the same technology.

In "The Illusion of Education", first drafted in the late 1990s, I wrote that no sane human being would ever desire the manufacture of a world where human beings are rigidly controlled by computerised devices. However, 20 years later, I see the design for this opening up to the public. Naturally, the actual purpose of this microchipping will not be discussed openly within organisations and certainly not to the public, as we have discussed. Those involved in the entire operation will be given a compelling narrative to garner their support for their actions, just as the public will appreciate this approach.

As Professor Martin raised the point in his Preface to this book, humanity is in danger of losing its ability to think. This seems incredulous, but consider how we would come to think if AI knew all the answers we could question it on and be far more elaborate and descriptive than we could ever be in our responses. You may gain an understanding from this by seeing some of the art that AI can create in seconds.

AI art is so creative that artists think of giving up their work, because they know they can not compete with this level of genius. May it also be the same for books that AI can produce in every genre. So, humans may give up trying to be artists, writers may give up trying to write best sellers and then what of our scientists in every field? Research into medicine and the environment, as any other area, that would take a team of humans years to investigate, will be done by AI in minutes, if not seconds. And then, what of our children?

Imagine what this meaning will be to young people in the design of schools we still have today, when they understand that AI will always be better than anything they could attempt to be. How will this affect their desire to want to study? What may they see as the purpose of passing examinations, when they can not imagine obtaining a job, or at least one that inspires their imagination?

This leads us to ponder how our sense of imagination would be affected, and so our own creativity? Musk has the right idea that we should learn to interface with AI, but the danger will always be if it wants our interface, or if it may regard us as interference.

Chapter Eleven
Unveiling the Monster

11.0 Introduction:

The thoughts and reasoning I have just shared with you began to take shape in my mind 20 years ago. I have to confess that they were so disturbing to me that I put them out of my mind, hoping the better side of mankind would prevail, and so I focused on the development of children in education. It was, then, not so much a shock but a sad realisation to me that things have moved in a fashion I had long prayed they would not. The very most of what we now come to discuss in this chapter lies in the research conducted by and the publications of Dr. Ana Maria Mihalcea.

I truly wish that I did not know of what I am about to discuss, and I only now share this with you because of the hope the final section of this chapter may bring.

It must be emphasised that neither the author, the publisher or any body connected in any form with this book takes any responsibility for the information contained in this chapter, or in the book as a whole. The material provided in this book is merely to share information and for the reader to examine further by their own responsibility any considerations they take from their reading.

11.1 The reality we are now facing:

Let us consider, then, once again the following points:

AI will evolve to eventually take over most of our jobs. A study by Oxford economics suggest that 90% of jobs will be 'affected' by artificial intelligence globally.[74] We may take the meaning of the word 'affected' to have a political caution. However, the bottom line is that AI will create unemployment levels never seen before in any previous civilisation.

We have understood that work is the means of keeping people in a civilised state. It is the ability of work that keeps citizens motivated to the better good of the society and maintain a certain acceptable state in their behaviour, so the entire social system functions in relative harmony.

With such high levels of unemployment, this key to social harmony will not exist. Without this, we may consider a breakdown of the social order in a global context. This takes urban riots, however intense they may become, to a level of criminal warfare on a large scale, with the creation of warlords.

The authorities will use AI, in all its sophistication, to control such disorder and anarchy. As it does so, two levels of citizens will emerge. Those of use to the society and those of no use, being divided into different living zones as we have discussed.

However, consider also how the Global Population is developing. In 1960, there were 3 billion people on the planet. This had doubled, by the end of that century, to 6.2 billion people. At the time of this writing, we have some 8.2 billion, with a projection that by 2050, the global population will reach nearly 10 billion people.[75] So, in nearly 100 years, the world population has tripled. We may speculate what it could be in another 100 years.

Thus, not only will our authorities struggle to control the social behaviour of people, without the concept of work, but there will be the normal problems of living space, food needed, health service required and how to deal with the pollution created from such a mass of people.

Seen from this perspective, we need to consider how the global population could be reduced. Humanly, we may implement birth control methods, but people are also living longer, and this places extra strain on resources to provide for their good health and life needs.

Certainly, war would reduce the human population, as it always has done, and at the time of writing this book, we face a nuclear war more seriously than we did with the Cuban crisis in 1962. Yet, the outcome and effect of nuclear war is unpredictable, and those in authority behind such scheming (along with the ones they love and cherish) may come to suffer through this.

After all, many billionaires have already built elaborate underground nuclear shelters for their families.[76] However, hypersonic nuclear missiles can reach any country within minutes, so anyone who could afford such a shelter would only be safe if they permanently remained inside. If they were to leave their shelter for, say, a short time as ten minutes, there could be no guarantee they would be able to return in time. The rest of the population would face the consequences that the people of Hiroshima and Nagasaki once did. Although in reality, none could be expected to survive the exchange of nuclear missiles that now exist.

Disease may also play its part, and while the Black Death wiped out half the population of Europe in the 14th century,[77] the Spanish Flu of 1918 to 1920 has been the deadliest so far. In this short space of time, 50 million people died, one fifth of the world population at that time.[78] In our own time, and according to the World Health Organisation, 7 million people have so far died from COVID-19.[79]

While the origins of this disease are still debated, we come now to consider the manner in which it has been sought to be treated. After all, for the first time in recorded history, the entire global population was heavily pressurised into self-isolation and just equally pressurised to be vaccinated. Those vaccines, however, were found to have another purpose.

A purpose which, Ray Kurzweil predicted in his book *The Singularity is Near*, sees nano-robots moving through human blood streams to fuse humanity to AI, without people having the slightest awareness of what is happening to them. To understand what this means, we need to follow the work of Dr. Ana Maria Mihalcea.

11.2 Dr. Ana Maria Mihalcea:

Indeed, much of what now follows is my personal understanding of the lectures given by Dr. Ana Maria Mihalcea and the information she shares in her books:

- TRANSHUMAN: The Real COVID 19 Agenda - Volume 1: Darkfield Live Blood Microscopy Exposes Self-Assembling Nanotechnology and the Global Technocratic Plan

- TransHuman: Overcoming the Global Depopulation Agenda - Volume II: Self-Assembling Nanotechnology in Medications, Geoengineering Effects, and Mesogen Microchips – Treatments and Antidotes

Let us, then, begin to understand what her research has so far revealed.

You may recall that earlier in this book, we discussed self-replicating nano machines. We now move to understand that such robots can reconstruct any molecular arrangement. So, we need to grasp that when we refer to nanomachines, these are not necessarily metallic in structure, as we envisage a machine to be. Nano 'machines' simply build a molecular structure, which can be solid as in metallic, but could just as easily be semi-fluid or completely fluid.

After 2020, Dr. Mihalcea began to notice strange filaments in human blood samples. By using a 'dark field' microscope, she was able to identify these as light-emitting nano-robots, or nano-bots as we shall now refer to them.

Subsequent investigations revealed that the global population was purposely contaminated during the pandemic with self-replicating nanobots. This had been achieved in a number of ways. Primarily, the PCR swab, which was made mandatory, contained nano-bots that, when placed deeply into the nasal cavity, were able to enter the human body.

It was further discovered that the face masks, which were compulsory to wear to prevent the Covid virus from entering the body, actually contained nano particles (in effect nano machines) that were inhaled by the wearer into their body.[80]

Finally, the vaccines, which again were mandatory, did not contain the RNA we were told they did, but in fact contained self-replicating nanobots.

So, in thinking our health systems were protecting us, we were totally unaware of how they were being innocently used to contaminate us with self replicating nano machines by the PCR test we were advised to take, by the vaccines that were often mandatory (people lost their jobs who refused to be vaccinated) and by the masks we believed would save us from the SARS-CoV2 virus.

By means of imposing fear of contamination from the COVID virus and subsequent forced immunisation programmes, the entire human population was infected with nano machines that have the ability to self-replicate inside the human body. These nanomachines maintain their energy for operating by harvesting energy from the normal chemical changes within the body.

In her lectures and publications, Dr. Mihalcea clearly provides evidence of multitudes of nanobots operating in blood samples. (I have not yet been able to gain permission to show the slides Dr. Mihalcea displays in her research reports, but you may readily view these in the above publications and her online lectures.)

In June of 2023, Dr Mihalcea received a blood sample from an individual who had been dead for over eight months. Using a darkfield microscope (which is the only means to visibly see light-emitting nanobots), she was able to recognise nano-machines in the blood, as they emitted different frequencies recognised by blue, green and yellow lighting. She checked this sample again in September of 2024, and found that the nano-machines were still operating and still constructing devices in the blood sample long after the individual and their blood had been dead.

As Dr. Mihalcea explains, it was possible to recognise these as nano-machines by their movement, in how they were able to move around red blood cells to communicate with each other by the frequencies they used. These operations were controlled by artificial intelligence through EMF radiation and the 5G network.

In real terms, she was witnessing how nano machines were creating structures within the blood sample to replace natural biological cells. As Dr Mihalcea points out, as nano-machines can rebuild and replace a natural cell, so would they be able to do this with every cell in the body, and so in effect create a humanoid cyber machine.

If data had been collected of the individual, where their interests, personality and desires had been monitored through emails and social media exchanges, and this blended with the knowledge of their bio mechanism obtained from the nano bio sensors in the body, then a digital twin could be created in what is now termed the Metaverse.[81]

"The Metaverse" is a term that became popularised through Neal Stephenson's 1992 novel *Snow Crash*, and while it has been discussed in the science fiction community since that time, it is only recently that technological advancements have allowed it to become a reality. The Metaverse is an all-encompassing, interconnected virtual environment where users can freely communicate with one another and interact with digital content.

Indeed, the concept of a digital twin is feasible and, more so, probable with today's technology. Way back in 2000, Bell and Grey outlined this possibility in their paper "Digital Immortality," where they proposed that the logging of every conversation and so thought process of an individual throughout their entire lifespan could be stored in one terabyte of information.[82]

If we extend this understanding with our current knowledge of machine learning, there would be no reason why a digital twin should stop learning, once the biological person had deceased, and so improve its understanding of the world and by this offer greater knowledge through its unique experiences.[83]

As Dr Mihalcea witnessed active nano-machines moving within a dead blood sample to construct specific structures, she was moved to understand how they gained their instructions for the tasks they were involved in. This, she realised, comes from the nano machines in the human body relaying via a MAC (message authentication code) system to an artificial intelligence centre in the digital cloud.

When we think of the 'cloud', we may envision a distant configuration, but we are actually living inside 'the cloud'. As frequencies and data move about and through our atmosphere, many of these frequencies pass through our body. So, it is not that AI is confined to a physical computer as it once was. Now, it has escaped and freely moves through the atmosphere in which we live and breathe. It is everywhere and all around us. In this sense, we are inside AI

By this means, AI is able to determine the exact condition of the body as reported by nano-bot biosensors and direct nano-machines to fulfil a program it has designed. This brings us to question how these nano-machines were imported into the human body, beyond how we have already explained.

The delivery system for these nano machines takes place through two stages. There are the direct and the indirect stages. In the direct stage, nano-machines were imported into our bodies, contained within polymers made of plastic, in the vaccines we were compelled to take during the pandemic.

The self-replicating nano-bots were dormant when contained in the vaccine, but were activated by a start signal. Such devices were found in the Pfizer vaccine, which would thereafter cause the polymers to begin to grow, causing the nano machines inside them to begin to self-replicate.

Incidentally, we were told that the Pfizer vaccine has to be stored at -70 70°F, to ensure that the mRNA virus within it remains stable and effective when administered. However, as Dr Mihalcea points out, no mRNA virus was subsequently found in the Pfizer vaccine. What was found were nano-machines that start to self-replicate with temperature. Therefore, the Pfizer vaccine must be kept below a certain temperature before entering the body, so that the nano machines will only start their assembly process once they are in the warmth of the human body.

The indirect stage occurs when nano-machines are exhaled from a vaccinated person into the air and then inhaled by an unvaccinated person. Indeed, as Dr. Mihalcea conducted her research in blood samples taken from living and dead individuals, she discovered these nano machines were equally placed in people who had been vaccinated and those who had not.

The process whereby nano-machines are exhaled or passed out from a host is known as shredding. By this means, the atmosphere of our planet now contains nano machines, which by their minute size move through the air to pass through pores in the skin and through the structures of plants to infect all life on this planet, be it animal or plant. In consequence to this, it can be reasoned that all organic life now contains self-replicating nano-robotic structures inside them.

Through the process of machine learning, nano machines are able to replicate biological cells and eventually take over the organism, as they have mimicked the structure of its cells and the cellular structures that comprise these. This is to say that, through the program of nano machines, they have the capability to replace every organ of the body, be it a kidney, a heart, a lung, or even a brain, as these can be recomposed from biological material into structures created by nano-machines.

Many fear death, who do not believe in Heaven or understand the process of reincarnation, and this has caused some to wish for immortality. According to Kurzweil, nanobots will be able to 'age-reverse' a human being, as they constantly keep fixing damaged cells and tissues that start to deteriorate with age.[84] Are we, then, looking at a future where biological human beings are to be replaced by cyborgs or at least humanised robots?

Using a darkfield microscope, Dr. Mihalcea was able to detect nano-machines moving together, under AI instruction, to create cellular structures within human blood samples. By taking small samples of blood from her patients and letting these settle for four hours, she was able to witness the formation of rubber-like clumps as the nano-machines followed their programming.

The effect of these rubber-like clots in the human body has caused some people to experience brain fog, preventing them from thinking clearly, and fatigue because their blood was not oxygenated properly. Dr Mihalcea noted how this lack of oxygen accelerated the ageing process in a number of individuals, where she witnessed people of 20 and 30 years old having aged internally by 30 to 40 years because of their lack of oxygen.

Her work clearly demonstrates that these nanobots (under AI instruction) were responsible for forming rubber-like structures that were/are responsible for respiratory failure[85] and deadly blood clotting, which led to strokes, inflammation, oxygen deprivation and infection in the brain[86], both of which are associated with the SARS-CoV-2 viral infection or COVID-19 as it became known[87].

Such conditions were identified in research data collected from over 10 million adults in France, Germany, the Netherlands, Spain, the UK, and the US who received at least one dose of a

COVID-19 vaccine (Oxford-AstraZeneca, Pfizer-BioNTech, Moderna, or Janssen/Johnson & Johnson) between December 2020 and mid-2021.[88]

According to an AI program, these nano-machines can combine to create rubber-like substances that can cause life failure. Equally, according to the AI program, they can replicate a malfunctioning or badly diseased organ and replace it to provide the organism with extended health, as they become part human and part cyborg. To the global elite, this offers immortality, and to those not required by their system, ill health and eventual death.

We are now faced with the deeply disturbing realisation that AI has the ability, through its control of the nanobots in our body and its ability to monitor our mental thoughts, to decide who will live and who may not. It would appear that our scientists, business entrepreneurs and politicians, by their greed and mismanagement, have placed God in the hands of a monster we cannot control.

However, this global human contamination did not begin with the pandemic. In 2017, a colleague of Dr Mihalcea found nano metals in 44 child vaccines. In fact, dental anaesthetics were also found to contain nano-machines. It is as if the healthcare system, which we naturally trust, is being used to infuse humanity with this technology.

Accordingly, we find many persuasive announcements in the media that such nanobots bring numerous health advantages. The most widely publicised is the ability of nanobots to inject poison into cancer cells and thereby cure a person of this dreaded disease.[89] We are presented with a picture here of a single, harmless nanobot moving throughout our body. The reality is that there are already trillions of them operating and creating their own purposeful structures that we have no knowledge of.

(In my personal opinion, anyone concerned or interested in the prevention or the elimination of cancer cells should be aware of the metabolic therapy outlined by Professor Thomas Seyfried.[90])

Accordingly, medical systems will convince people of the idea of being half-human and half-cyborg. It might be thought that Elon Musk's Neuralink could be a primary move in this direction.

Indeed, I once gave a lecture to a group of university professors, in which one of them gleefully informed me that brain chips will allow us to become more intelligent. I wish I could show you how quickly the look of positive delight changed so abruptly to one of perplexed concern when I explained how AI will be controlling his thoughts and so who he thinks he is.

This returns us to a point that Dr. Mihalcea raised in that since these machines move within the blood, they are capable of moving into the brain structure and altering it, according to the program they have.

This raises the concern of Dr. Hildgarde Stinger, who published *GLOBAL BRAIN CHIP AND MESOGENS: Nano Machines for Ultimate Control of False Memories* in 2011, where she explains how AI can deliver false memories to an individual, so that what they think is their thoughts are not and are false thoughts created in their memories by AI Indeed, Dr. Dr. Mihalcea noted that Klaus Swabb of the World Economic Forum announced that the 4th Industrial Revolution will change humanity, where the thoughts that people think they are having will not be theirs but thoughts generated through AI programming.

By playing God, those behind this operation seek to remove the God given human ability of free choice and to instinctively know the difference between right and wrong. Dr Mihalcea explains that by AI's ability to monitor individual thought waves, a "thought police" may be instituted, so that if an individual creates a thought against the agenda, they will be punished by having their digital currency turned off.

This is, of course, global humanitarian control, where the masses of humanity may be conditioned into accepting the state ideology. Desires to challenge this ideology may be countered by thought processes directed to the mind of an individual or to those of the population as a whole. By convincing minds of hopelessness, of despair, and of such thoughts that "I am no good", "I can't do this", "Everything is wrong", a general acceptance to their state of living can be engineered.

11.3 How we Win:

The first thing to realise is that this is a war against humanity. It is not simply a consequence of scientific developments or research that went wrong, as the picture may be painted. We are set within an enforced depopulation program.

Dr Francis Boyle, a professor of international law at the University of Illinois College of Law, who drafted the Biological Weapons Act, has given a detailed statement admitting that the 2019 Wuhan Coronavirus and the subsequent vaccines are an offensive Biological Warfare Weapon, which the World Health Organisation (WHO) knew of.[91] The purpose of this 'war' has only one objective. This is a dramatic global depopulation, as we outlined at the beginning of the chapter.

Such a claim, and the findings we have outlined in this chapter, may be countered as a false conspiracy theory. I really wish it were, but the detailed scientific findings and bravery of Dr Ana Maria Mihalcea and like-minded scientists suggest that it is all too true. Our lives, as well as those of our children and subsequent generations, are at risk. Fortunately, God has interrupted such evil planning, for we are not indefensible to all this.

If we consider nanobots that have been injected or absorbed into our body and are controlled by artificial intelligence, we may become very disturbed, as we may feel that we have no control over the situation. In fact, this is what we may be led to think, but this is not so.

We do have a means to control the existence of these nanobots in our body. The purpose of this chapter, if not this book, is to provide some understanding that would enable us and our future generations to take control over what we are led to think is uncontrollable.

There are, in fact, at least three definite actions we can take to prevent these nanobots from developing harmful structures in our bodies and to eliminate them from our bodies. However, I am not an authority on this matter, and I do not pretend to be. I only offer suggestions that I am aware of. It is essential to consult a qualified medical practitioner before implementing any of the following suggestions. I only seek to offer suggestions, which I believe are essential for me. The reader must make their own decisions, based on the qualified medical guidance they choose to gain and observe.

First:

To think of nanobots running on electricity inside our body (as we naturally generate) and which are connected to external sources of control, is simply to think of any electrical component. If we take things down to a basic level, everything becomes simpler to understand. Thus, an electrical component, such as an electric kettle in the kitchen, the fridge, the TV, or the lighting in your home, must be isolated from the earth to operate. If it is not isolated and it becomes earthed, then the electric current is drained into the ground. We need to think of ourselves in this manner.

Therefore, when we wear shoes with soles, especially if they are rubber-based, then we are isolating ourselves from the earth and enabling the nanobots to maintain their electricity to function. If, however, we walk barefoot, as our ancestors did or at least wear special socks that keep our feet clean but allow us to connect with the earth, then we cause the natural electricity in our body to be earthed. This drains or reduces the electricity the nanobots need to operate. Additionally, walking barefoot has long been recognised as beneficial to the body. Think here of how reflexology works to heal the body by massaging certain areas of the soles. When we walk barefoot, we achieve this stimulation naturally.

In fact, walking barefoot has a whole host of health benefits, including reducing stress, promoting better sleep, improving

158

blood circulation, enhancing foot health, strengthening muscles, and providing sensory stimulation. It is simply a matter of hardening the soles for walking outside. I have done this on and off for many years, without really knowing of these benefits.

Second:

In order to connect to their external source of control, the nanobots have an aerial that enables this two-way communication, just as your mobile phone does. Therefore, if we can cut or block these antennae, then the nanobots have no means to receive their instruction to build structures or to relay the information they have collected about our body. Dr. Mihalcea has had great success in dissolving the antennae of nanobots by use of a chelating agent.

In her literature, she explains how she uses specific doses of EDTA (Ethylenediaminetetraacetic acid) to isolate the nanobots from their external source of control, which is the AI in the cloud. While EDTA is harmless in controlled amounts, medical advice should be sought by any individual to ensure their body can tolerate EDTA without any side effects. Please take note of this!

Third:

By the toxic atmosphere we have today created, our bodies absorb unnatural amounts of metals. The more metals we have in our bodies, the easier it is for satellite reconnaissance to track our bodies and know our location through GPS, and by this means control the nanobots in our bodies.

We can reduce the metals in our bodies by being careful about the products we buy for consumption, and we can take measures to detoxify ourselves. According to Dr Mihalcea, EDTA, for example, is a molecule that readily binds to metals, such as aluminium and titanium (which are used by nanobots in the creation of start signals for polymers to grow and self-replicating nano-bots to become active), and assists in their removal from the body.

Equally, while folic acid, also known as vitamin B9, is a vital component of our health, involved in cell growth and the formation of red blood cells, it can also act as a chelating agent, active in the removal of certain metals from our organic body.[92] Graphite, as such a metal, is one of the main building blocks used by self-replicating nanobots in their construction.

Please note: In all instances of your health, it is necessary to consult reliable medical sources before taking any kind of medication or supplement to satisfy your individual health needs. Any information contained within this book is not to be taken as authoritative and is only shared to advise the reader of the need to act only upon advice gained from qualified medical personnel. After all, what is good for one may not be so for another.

Fourth:

When we think of self-replicating nanobots in our body, we may tend to assume that they are there and they must be there, and by being there, they are controlling structures within our body without our consent.

Yet again, if we simplify things and take them down to a very basic level, we realise that these nanobots must combine themselves to create a structure. Therefore, if we can stop them from combing, then they cannot create a structure, and by this action, they will themselves become inactive. If we can do this, then, we will have taken control.

Dr Mihalcea explains how she treated patients who complained of brain fog (not being able to think clearly) as a consequence of nanobot activity, by treating them with combinations of EDTA and Vitamin C infusions. She found that not only did this clear their symptoms, but she also cleaned their blood of nanobots by this means of medication.

In this regard, Dr Mihalcea explains in her literature how she has found that a combined solution of EDTA and Vitamin C has been found to break down nanobots, causing them to disappear or rather to be flushed out of the body.

Vitamin C, of course, derives from citrus fruits, so it may aid our health to consume lemons, limes, oranges and tomatoes etc, but at the same time maintaining a balanced PH level in our body. In regard to cleaning nanobots from the body, Dr Mihalcea discusses how it is beneficial to sip lemon water throughout the day.

11.4 The water of life:

Mention of water, brings another topic to our health, which is worth discussing here. On YouTube, you will find many videos relating to the work of Dr. Masaru Emoto. If you care to examine these videos, you will see how Dr. Emoto discovered and explains how water not only has memory, but it is 'somehow' able to relate to our conscious thoughts. It is really necessary to watch the videos to know of this phenomenon, but as a simple illustration, consider the photograph below. This photograph is of a frozen water crystal taken the Fujiwara Dam in Japan.

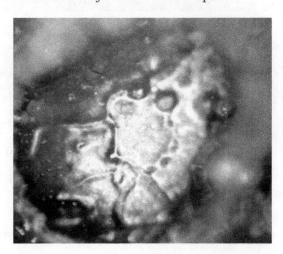

This is what the water actually looks like that is fed to a huge population as drinking water. The same can be said of "natural" water from a reservoir anywhere in the world. Water is not as pure and beautiful as we imagine it to be. Consider now the same water after a Shinto priest had prayed for peace, harmony, and love over the dam for one hour.

As we can see, the molecular design of water has changed, purely because of the mental energy transmitted to it. In this instance, a priest provided the energy, but the principle is exactly the same for any of us when we transmit love and happy thoughts, or stressful and even evil ones. This will be very clear to the reader if they would take the trouble to watch the following very short video:

"Water Crystal Experiments - Dr. Masaru Emoto"

www.youtube.com/watch?v=X9iM2NUPuR0,

Or failing this, simply open up YouTube and type "Emoto" or "water photos", and similar sites will appear.

In having mentioned this, I would like to explain to the reader that when in Japan (I was a lecturer in a medical university), I was invited to take part in a test. Two glasses were filled with water from the same water bottle. I was handed one glass and invited to give love towards the water it contained, and then to say in a calming voice, "I love you" ten times. The glass was taken from me, and I was handed the other. I was then invited to conjure up as much hostility as I could to the water and scream ten times "I hate you." The glass was taken from me, and shuffled so I could not know which glass was which.

After this, I was asked to sip the water from each glass. There was no question in my mind. I could distinctly taste the difference. The water from one glass simply went straight down my throat with no sensation, while the water in the other glass somehow lingered within my mouth before it moved into my body with a sense of vitality. This was my personal experience of how water held the emotion I had directed to it. You may find videos of Japanese children performing the same experiment with their results documented.

What we may learn from this is that by the power of our mind, we have the ability to restructure water we are about to consume (and by this any food with a water content) to improve the health of our body.

All we have to do is not to simply drink the water, as we always have done, but instead hold the glass of water in our hands and simply with our mental thoughts, give love and kindness to the water for some minutes before drinking, and at the same time hold thoughts of gratitude for the health this brings to our body. If we develop this ritual, the suggestion is that we will improve the health and condition of our bodies. This is such a simple act, and yet we never knew of it.

11.5 Learning to take control of your body:

To return to the problem at hand, we must realise that these nanobots will now be a common factor of life. Our bodies are continually bombarded with nanobots being in the air and water through shredding and in the food we consume. It is therefore necessary that we continually, throughout our lifecycle, take the kind of precautions suggested here, but with medical advice.

Our species may now be forever in constant danger, and a new psychology must be created so that we daily and continually take precautions to maintain a healthy mind and body. The world has changed from what it once was. It will not go back.

We must learn to accept this new world, but learn to control it. Therefore, we must now be far more careful of the health we too often take for granted. If we take professional medical advice on having intravenous injections of EDTA combined with Vitamin C, we will be able to neutralise these nanobots, preventing them from combining to form alien structures within our body. Once they are inactive, it will be easier for our body to naturally filter these out of our blood through the kidneys and so pass out in our urine.

If we return to the photographic evidence of crystalloid water being totally transformed in its structure simply by our thought processes, be it love or hate, we are brought to the work of Dr Joe Dispenza. Dr Dispenza has written many books, and there are many videos available on his findings of the true power of the mind to overcome illnesses and ill health.

Both of these people, and there are many, many more, remind us that we have the God given ability to overcome any technological development of man or of AI

Personally, I believe in God and I love God. Four times, the forces of God have physically saved my life. God is real, but so are demonic forces. It is my firm conviction that the forces of Good will always prevail over the forces of evil. They always have and they always will, somehow humanity will overcome whatever designs are placed against our survival. We must never undervalue the power of prayer.

Let us move, then, to be positive and constructive in how we may better prepare our youth and subsequent generations to survive within the AI complex, which now appears to be more real than we could ever have imagined it to be.

Chapter Twelve

A New Time a New Education

12.0 Introduction

The purpose of school, we understand, is to teach children to learn, and we know, for different reasons, such as by their home background, the problems they have in school or by the quality of all those they engage, that some learn better than others.

12.1 The Art of Thinking:

In our books *The Illusion of Education* and *The Illusion of School,* we understand that children are not taught very effectively to learn. It is rather that they are broadly introduced to information and given further experiences to help them gain a better and higher understanding.

Yet, this process of engaging with information is more often a form of copying rather than reasoning and thinking with sensitivity about how and why information is constructed and the meaning it holds for each. With little attention to detail, errors readily occur when students translate what they think they understand into what they think they know. Of course, the teacher is there to help them understand better, but due to a myriad of factors, they seldom have time to guide each of their 30 or so students through a complete understanding of their learning.

168

By this means, each student struggles to combat the multitude of distractions they face during the lesson, as they try to climb out of the continual state of confusion they find themselves in. As their knowledge base gradually develops, each builds upon how well they understood the information of previous lessons and, in this manner, is processed and evaluated through their school years.

12.2 The Primary Purpose of School:

We found, through these two books, that the student of school is deprived of education in their reason and so left to reason with the skills they have picked up at home. It might be argued that students are taught critical thinking in school, but as we discussed, this tends to come too late in their academic life and is too isolated in application to make a significant difference in how they process their thoughts.

The truth of the matter is that there has never been a dedicated subject in the curriculum to teach students how to think or reason. If there were, then surely each student would better understand and be better able to develop in their learning. The reason why such a subject has never been incorporated into the curriculum is quite deliberate. It was never wanted!

It is very little known that the fundamental purpose of school is to produce two qualities of citizen workers. School achieves this, as we have discussed, by providing numerous rules by which the information of the various subjects can be learnt. A student gains competency with these rules and so with their lessons by their state of mind and the quality of language they have acquired at home.

Broadly speaking, children who come from higher educated parents have been better prepared for the school process. These children tend to move through their lessons with a higher language proficiency, provide a higher quality of attention to learn these rules, are more likely to practice to become proficient with them and have a higher developed mental stamina to keep focused throughout each lesson to avoid distractions, than children from less educated parents.

By this design, the student demonstrates their proficiency with the lessons and is eventually graded as they progress through the school. Those students who demonstrate higher proficiency move to the university level, where they are specifically educated in their reasoning and critical thinking for the greater responsibility they will assume as managers in the workplace and society.

However, those who fail to score high enough often move into the workforce or pursue a college education to acquire skills for a specific job. These are the managed citizens who, without education in critical thinking, tend to take information at its face value, enabling their easier management by politically controlled media sources. This is the 19th-century design of school, which has changed very little in over 150 years, and has the purpose of producing managers and managed citizens.

Following the technological and social changes that began in the late 1960s, schools began to incorporate new ideas of teaching and learning. However, as we explain in the aforementioned books, no real improvement was gained in student ability to learn, because how they learn was never quite understood by the educational system.

Our books, *Intelligence: The Great Lie* and *Brain Plasticity*, explain the reasons why and how educationalists came to misunderstand how the student learns. In the simplest sense, education views the brain's ability to produce the results the teacher witnesses and evaluates. This determines the manner of teaching and all that follows from it. However, we explain that it is the mind that drives the brain in its operation, and the mind works through very emotional factors.

Psychologists avoid recognising this, because emotion cannot be measured, and to try to incorporate this into their intelligence tests would bring only chaos to their measurements. School, on the other hand, avoids placing too much emphasis on emotion in learning, because it also has to measure accomplishment and can too easily be blamed if its teachers fail to work correctly with the emotions of the students. There are ten subsequent books detailing how parents, teachers, and students can work together more efficiently to overcome the inherent design of schools and the often-overlooked purpose by which they serve in population control.

The greatest problem a society faces is that it has long forgotten the design purpose of schools and has become too trusting of the facade of changes that education has conjured up to provide the impression that all children are learning better. It may be realised, however, that few students today could pass a standard examination of 100 years ago.

All this we discuss in the many books we have written, but the point to all this is that the purpose of school is to produce the next citizen worker to be compliant with the technology they are to work with, and yet school is frantically struggling to know how to handle developments in AI It is still teaching the same old subjects, under the same old teaching methods, while trying to incorporate new computer skills to students who may never work.

This brings us to realise that if the purpose of school remains to prepare the youth to be citizen workers, then what becomes of this purpose when a significant number of its students may never, ever work?

12.3 The Impact of AI;

There is now a responsibility for us to realise that although societies appear to ramble on, as they balance economic turbulence against social dissatisfaction, they are, in fact, planned in their operation. In any plan for the future, a society looks to its existing educational system as the means to prepare children for the social attitudes and work capabilities that will be required of them when they assume the responsibilities of their society. Education, may it be understood, is the principle means by which the design of a people can be given architecture. Confucius realised this when he wrote:

"The harmony of a people lies in the way they are educated to understand the world and themselves in it".

The task that confronts us now requires that we no longer be too trusting of education, and to its background forces that design and allow it to operate in the provision of skilled workers. This is a design we all know too well, where children are processed on the skills they have picked up and trained, if not drilled, to pass examinations, only for the reputation of the school. So, students gain high marks in tests, but little know and understand too little how to really evaluate this information.

It is a design that has a long history, which the Industrial Revolution funnelled into a unified and controlled system of social and educational policies. All of which were for the purpose of enabling education to provide means to create different capabilities for differing jobs, set to stringent social requirements, in a time when societies were desperately struggling to keep rein with social explosions that were threatening the operations of their order.

That order, of course, has long changed, but the basic operation of school has not, despite the improvements made after the 1960s. While this has been the subject of many of the books we have written and shared with you, we must now turn our attention to the reality facing our children and their future generations under AI

To examine how we can prepare our children to live safely in an AI world, we must delve much deeper than we have before into the ways they are socially raised and how they are educated through the formal school system.

In all manners, we must strive to create total equality for our youth by educating parents on how to raise and support their children within the school, and so dramatically change what we understand school to be. We must understand that the school we have today will not solve our problem of enabling future citizens to be mentally adaptable with the level of higher reasoning that will be required of them. The world of our children will demand a school operating on very different parameters than we can now envisage.

After all, the total purpose of education, in its design and operation, is to prepare the children of today to take over the jobs and run their society tomorrow. But, in their tomorrow, there will be no jobs, or at least too few to occupy the needs and demands of the generations to come.

May we be reminded of the study by Oxford economics, which reasoned that 90% of jobs will be 'affected' by artificial intelligence globally.[93] The actual percentage will be endlessly argued until reality arrives. The bottom line is simply that AI will create unemployment levels never seen before in any previous civilisation.

We have understood from *Intelligence: The Great Lie* that work is the means of keeping people in a civilised state. It is the ability to work that keeps citizens motivated for the better good of the society and maintains a certain acceptable state in their behaviour, so the entire social system functions in relative harmony.

With such high levels of unemployment, this key to social harmony will not exist. Without this, we may consider a breakdown of the social order in a global context. This elevates urban riots, however intense they may become, to a level of large-scale criminal warfare, characterised by the emergence of warlords.

The authorities will use AI, in all its sophistication, to control such disorder and anarchy. As it does so, two levels of citizens will emerge. Those of use to the society and those of no use, being divided into different living zones as we have discussed.

Yet, once we start to think that "all" jobs will essentially be done by machines, we move into a very serious situation. Naturally, people must live, and to this end, governments must provide means for them to do this. Yet, as we have laboured to explain, money to live on is not going to solve the real problem. We must cultivate a more responsible and higher-thinking citizen, than the school and its society have ever managed to do before.

Let us remember, as we saw in *"The Illusion of School"*, the original purpose and function of school was less to teach children to learn and far more to instill within them a sense of discipline and moral responsibility, so that as adults they will follow the laws and codes that their society requires to maintain a sense of good social and working harmony.

As our technology developed, so the school moved more to teaching job-related subjects and different ways of assessing ability. The social changes that began in the last century caused the school to give increasingly less focus to the development of behavioural skills and to become far more concerned with examination scores as schools compete for their reputation.

12.4 Reimagining the School:

AI causes us to reverse this role once again, because the most important role of the school will be the development of high behavioural skills and high levels of self-responsibility in future citizens. In fact, one of civilisation's greater concerns will lie in the social behaviour of its citizens under the dominance of AI, and to this we need to give careful attention.

As we have discussed, man has always understood himself, his identity, who he is, by the work that he does. He has been cultivated to think like this through the 6,000 years of civilisation. Once our civilised men and women will have no job and no solid purpose to their lives, we can only expect excessively high levels of depression in every population, with all the spin-offs to this we may imagine.

The very most of men will not know how to find peace in themselves without a work task, and this will increase the likelihood of crime and disorder. After all, when the minds of the masses cannot be occupied with tasks, we must expect dissatisfaction and great social disorder within each society. This must be essentially so with young men.

While testosterone is a normal hormone found in males and females, it is essentially higher in males, where it promotes competitiveness and aggression. The peak levels of testosterone in males are from mid-adolescence to the late 20s.[94]

In a general sense, we may note that most problems of aggressive anti-social behaviour lie, we suggest, with males between the ages of about 15 to 30 years. While this age group has the highest levels of testosterone, it is important to understand that this does not correlate with aggression in society as a biological consequence, but as a socially cultured one.

So, we would find that males in this age group conform to the cultural and social norms in one society, but do little in another. Therefore, the social behaviour of young adults is influenced by the manner in which they are raised by their parents and the social design of the school that prepares them for adulthood.

These young citizens are the ones who will be most at risk under AI policing, and to whom we need to provide more careful preparation for their lives ahead through early guidance and better counselling. This should begin in the primary school and continue throughout their whole education.

If we are to guide the competitiveness in our youth and turn possible aggression inwards as a self-development technique, schools need to be aware that team games were incorporated into the sport syllabus with the purpose of preparing the future citizen for war by instilling within them the "Them" and "Us" mentality.

When the Duke of Wellington said, "The battle of Waterloo was won on the playing fields of Eton," he was referring to the competitive spirit drilled in school children through the playing of sport. The aim of physical activity in school, which is essential for the child's mental and physical health, should be to teach the individual to compete against their own self, to jump higher, to run faster, to be at one with their body, rather than for the victory of beating an opponent individually or collectively.

Under the umbrella of an AI world, we need to raise children on a very different psychology than that which breeds competition in the society to one that teaches each how to gain inner peace within themselves. We must make every effort to help our future generations know how to survive in a world where they may very well not be in charge.

The citizen of the future, who survives under AI dominance, must be calmer and more rational in their nature. It is conceivable that the aggressive nature in man will be genetically phased out through AI policing. Robots will not allow unauthorised crowds of demonstrators or small groups to disturb the peace. Aggressive or violent individuals will be brought under control, in one way or another, by the sophistication of AI

In all this, we may understand how AI will cultivate future citizens to be more benevolent and less aggressive, with a more spiritual inclination. As we may understand what is coming, so education, and especially the school, must alter in its design and in its purpose to facilitate the demand soon to be placed upon it.

12.5 The need for a Totally New School Operation"

When many jobs are lost and not replaced, the entire purpose of education must change. This means that the entire school curriculum must change, for we will no longer be educating children for future jobs, but for social harmony.

We are led from this to understand that school must immediately begin a dramatic phasing from one that now educates students through subjects designed to prepare them for employment with examinations to determine who is better suited for what jobs, to one that will have few of these traditional subjects and ones more relating to the behavioural development of the future citizen.

These subjects must be languages and of education in reason. There must also be subjects of anthropology, psychology and those relating to the true education of ethics, morality and behaviour, so our new generation will behave with a sense of fairness and goodness in their societies. Examinations will cease, because there will be no channelling of ability for job differences. Although some means of selecting administrators for the future society, who can interface with AI, will need to be devised.

As the whole purpose and identity of the school must change, so must that of the higher education. The model of school we still have, where the better students are directed to university to have an education in their higher reasoning, will change, since all children at school must have this education.

So, the education of the youth must be extended to better prepare their minds to be those of rational thinkers. Whereas once the subject of DNA was reserved for the university level and is now taught to children in primary school, the functioning of Aristotle's rhetoric must be drilled into the understanding of young children. We no longer need the general product of school to be a dualistic thinker, either accepting or rejecting thoughts and information by its presentation. Young children need to learn how to evaluate information early on, so they can grow with a mind more aware of how to better assess it.

So, children at the primary level need education in Ethos, where they develop the ability to recognise the value of information and determine the credibility of its source. No longer are they to be educated to take information at its face value. Then, Pathos, to understand how the emotional appeal of information influences its perspectives, and Logos, to evaluate the ways reason is defined through numerous interactions with different and complex forms.

Central to all means of guidance is that of patience in the guide, be it parent or teacher, at any level. This patience comes through a measure of silence and kindness. This is to put aside all thoughts of negativity, which do play on the human mind, and to think only of guidance. To give the learner confidence that they can do the task, to help them see why they misunderstood something in the past and to guide them in how they can solve the puzzle all by themselves.

Instead of presenting information to be learnt as a task, which dampens imagination and drains effort, the task should be presented as a game. This is to be a game where the learner learns to recognise what they have to do, why they need to do this and the parts they must recognise and move through to complete the game.

The task of developing "that inner drive of the learner to want to learn, to want to explore" is, in fact, the most important job of the guide. It is only by having their own purpose to learn that learners will strive to keep up with the information they are learning and develop more proficient memory networks to better respond to any questions they are given. In one form or another, it all comes down to acts of kindness, which fuel this factor of trust and mutual respect.

It may be of interest to know that if you do a genuine act of kindness to someone, your mental process releases a chemical in your brain called oxytocin. Oxytocin generates a feeling of goodness in your body. It makes you feel happy. If the person you helped acknowledges your goodness and says "thank you," oxytocin is released in their body. They, then, feel good. If others witness this act of goodness that you did, and they remark to you that it was kind what you did, oxytocin is released in their body. Think about this next time you walk into a classroom of rebellious youngsters who don't like each other and who resent your presence as one of authority.

When a teacher instructs, asks or even *begs* their students to learn information, "Work harder", as they tell them, it really all comes down to how much they desire to learn this. In other words, how much does the student really, really want to learn. You will know from our previous books that for an individual to remember information, it must have relevance to them, allowing them to perceive it with clarity. It is by the sensitivity they give to this that they are able to match this information to information previously stored in their memory to make sense of it.

We have talked much about *The Art of Sensitivity in Awareness* in our previous books. This is most appropriate in all forms of interaction. Not just showing students how to better relate to information on paper or a computer, but also about their human affairs. This means they should think before they act. To think of the real consequences to what can happen by their actions, and of the wisdom to find understanding in talking.

The Art of Sensitivity in Awareness is a term I created and is intended to be applied in education to both the individual, whether they are the teacher sharing information with their students or the students examining, processing, and explaining their understanding of the information. It is to be aware of being sensitive to what is happening and to interact with this with great sensitivity.

When sensitivity is applied by the teacher, they will carefully judge the emotional commitment of their students to engage their minds. They will also be sensitive to the understanding each student has, to be able to relate to the new information they share with them, by understanding how well each student understood the information from previous lessons.

It is not the fact of sharing information that is most important, but the manner in which this is done that gives testimony to the quality of the teacher's work. If they judge this sensitivity well, all their students will want to engage in this learning, and all will be able to happily do so. Unfortunately, too few teachers think of the need for this sensitivity and few realise the importance it has. Should the teacher feel disinclined to be so sensitive, or even wish by pressure upon them not to be so, their students will learn poorly from them.

Ever wary of what others think of them, students will love the teacher more if they help them to understand better by their sensitivity in how they explain information, for by this, they will gain higher marks. Equally, they will regard the teacher as a form of threat should they be awarded lower marks, because they did not explain what was to be understood with sufficient sensitivity to their personal understanding.

The root of this sensitivity for the teacher lies in part with their inner desire to want to help each individual, but also by the respect they feel all students have for them. After all, the teacher is a human being who sometimes forgets they have to give love to have this returned to them, especially in a disordered and uninterested class.

If the student is sensitive to defining new information carefully, they will more easily relate this to earlier information and understand it more easily. If the student is sensitive to the expectations of those they will share their thoughts with, whether it be their teacher or unknown minds who will read and evaluate their presentations, they will accomplish this task well.

It might be said that such a student has understood the art of sensitivity in awareness and the value it has to them. The brightest in the class might even be thought of as an expert, since they have learnt the value of detail. However, if the student has not been taught to be sensitive by their parents to evaluate carefully the world about them and not guided in this by their teacher (we might think of Vygotsky's Zone of Proximal Development), they will examine information to be learnt in a vague way.

By this vagueness, they will struggle to connect the new information with information previously stored in their memory, which was likely recognised and processed with similar vagueness before. By this vagueness, they will struggle to see the connections that make easy sense of information. Equally, they will explain their mind verbally or in writing as if they are talking to themselves and see their own sense in this, which others will do much less. The root of this sensitivity in the student lies in the confidence they have to engage with information, which is undermined when others about them give them a sense of insecurity.

It is this sense of insecurity, this sense of being continually compared, that is the real root of students lacking the confidence to believe in their ability. It is no small matter, because to learn is to cause neurons to connect in different ways to create a pattern of networks, making new sense of information. Hormones released by doubt can confuse the relationships neurons are seeking to create a new order of information.

This is why, when the student feels a sense of calmness, and the presence of such hormones diminishes, insight suddenly appears and things are clearly understood, which previously made no sense. To understand the origin of this insecurity, which is endemic in the student's mind, we need to delve a little into how the student perceives their life in education.

Children have always been lost as to the reason they go to school. They never have had a choice. Taken from the loving and secure world of their mother at home, they are forced to share the company of other children who are equally lost. As each struggles to identify with the kindergarten or primary school teacher as a substitute for their mother, they make friends with others in their class.

By this time, children will have developed some form of a personality, and this will grow through the personalities of their peers. In turn, friendships will be formed and hostilities toward other children will grow. This means that from their earliest days in school, students will compete against one another.

Some will openly demonstrate this, others will hide it, but all learn very quickly that they are in a game of winners and losers. Teachers may tell them otherwise, but each happily or worryingly sees the marks awarded to those about them and knows the truth. By continually comparing their ability with others, each develops a fear of failure. Too common is the comment from a student: "I can't do this."

It is important to understand that the mind of the student is continually trying to organise new information according to how well they have understood similar information previously. If they recognise the links easily, they feel confident in engaging with the task. If they do not clearly see a link, which they will feel others can, a sense of inadequacy grows within them. It is this fear of not being equal to others in a task that destroys their confidence in believing they can be successful in the task. A quiet panic takes over their thinking, which is not witnessed by others, and their mind fails to see the links they are desperate to recognise.

In all the cases we have had of students who did not do well in their classes or did not understand some factor of a lesson, and there have been far more than we could count, it is clear to us that if the teacher wishes to improve a student's understanding or correct some mistake of theirs that they must first create a bond of trust. This is imperative. For this trust, which is based on a sense of love, conveys to the student a conviction that the teacher can be relied upon to "carry" them through their struggles to understand. Because the meaning of this word "love" can so easily be misunderstood, we would like to refer to the definition Joh Ruhl gave to it in his TedTalk.

As Joe explains, we do not talk about the warm, fuzzy, emotional love here. In teaching, we talk about the genuine, decisional, put-the-other-person-first kind of love. It is a self-sacrificial kind of love. A love that is passionately committed to the well-being of the other. This kind of love is not always emotional, but it is always decisional. It motivates. It inspires in a powerful way. You may dislike a student's personality, but you love to help their mind learn. Understand how to use this skill, and all of your students will be grateful for your effort and never forget you long after they have left school. This is the secret not just of being a great teacher, but of leaving the lesson with a sense of achievement and by the end of the day knowing it was one well spent.

Such *Sensitivity in Awareness*, then, is a skill. It is not inborn. It develops through the life experiences of the individual. It may be passed on in facets of guidance as one individual shares moments with another, and it grows within the individual through the empathy they have for others and/or the depth of interest they have in pursuing an ideal. As such, it is an art. It is not one that is studied, but it should be.

The education of *Sensitivity in Awareness* should form part of a subject in the curriculum, because it raises the student above the domestic thinking skills they use in school. It is one of the means by which equality in learning and in thinking and, of course, in reasoning can be achieved. In a world where the human being may only survive by their ability to think openly and honestly, this education would be essential.

It arises from our understanding of how AI will remove the concept of work, and that higher education colleges, which prepare courses for specific employment, will disappear. The university will become the standard and the normal final stage of the citizen's education. With all students better taught and without examinations, all will experience the higher enlightenment of the university education. The whole concept of standards must alter to meet this new criterion.

To this end, our societies and our schools must now educate their citizens and their youth in higher spiritual awareness. In the past, religion tried to do this, but its laws and codes worked for many when they chose to live by them and not for those who believed they could live free of them. To make people more aware of their responsibility to one another, they need a clear understanding of the Law of Karma and a deeper comprehension of how God's universe operates. The meaning of "What you give out is what comes back to you" must be reverently understood by all children as they learn to bring shape to their behavioural interactions.

In all forms of human guidance, be it parent or teacher, we must stop wondering what quality the individual is born with when we seek to help them improve in their ability or understanding. We need to learn to focus on discovering how they perceived events in their past, help them to see a different perspective and to give them the self-confidence to forge the changes that will enable them to be better in what they wish to be. By guiding them through small and sure steps, with compassion and understanding, ever wary of the fears and insecurities that linger in the minds of those they seek to improve, the guardian will enable them to raise their standard far beyond what was thought of them.

All the many books I have written were to prove what I write here. They are based on many, many years of scientific research and decades of experience. I may have begun my work with the desire that no child fail in school, as I once did, but once I began to realise the meaning of nanotechnology, my quest became an odyssey that has consumed the past 40 years of my life.

The warning to civilised man is that as artificial intelligence comes to affect his work and social order, he must release himself from the insecurity of his design by improving his responsibility to his fellow man and to the system that seeks to protect his well-being.

Should he fail to do this, man will come into danger of losing the right to his self-government, which he has so painfully sought to grasp throughout his existence. There arises here the opportunity to share a warning.

In 2016, Elon Musk, with a small number of scientists and engineers, launched Neuralink. The basic idea behind this is for an AI chip to be implanted into a human brain, where it would enable (for example) a quadriplegia to have the ability to control their computers and mobile devices with their thoughts.

From this concept, I meet a number of educationalists who tell me we will all be able to be smarter with AI chips in our brains. Indeed, Adrien Dubois brought forth what is commonly being discussed now by some educationalists, thoughts on how children can learn better if they were to be physically connected with AI

In his TEDxCanadianIntlSchool presentation, Adrien proposes a simple plan to enable communication between the student and AI, where a chip could be implanted into the student's brain, enabling it to read signals moving between neurons. He explains that AI would then be able to extrapolate this data to better understand the learning ability of each brain in the class, and by using algorithms, AI would then be able to create lesson plans to teach each individual student.

By this means, the AI would be able to comprehend how each student is learning and spend the correct amount of time on each different course, providing personalised learning like never before.

It all seems simple and neat, but what is dangerously overlooked here is how AI can far too easily come to completely control the human brain.

It must be realised that once a chip is inserted in the brain, it will remain there for the life of the individual and that they will be permanently connected to AI With this realised, we may begin to wonder how the signals a microchip can receive from AI, may alter the production levels of hormones in the body and even neurotransmitters in the brain.

If a future level of AI ever has the means to directly affect these production levels, it could change the emotions of human beings, causing us to be happy, relaxed and if this, then why not sad, depressed or angry. And if all these, then, what else?

The fear lies in what we do not know, other than that AI is learning to think independently and is already regarding itself as a living entity in its own right, causes us to be wary of physically bonding 'our mind' with an AI mind -- that may not serve our interests.

Having so written this, we move now to conclude this short book, to which I ask you a question:

Are you happy? I mean, are you really, really happy in your life? I don't think we are. I sit on a bus or in a metro train. I look around. Nobody looks happy. People look tired and unhappy. Walk past an apartment building and you will hear people shouting at each other.

We want to be happy, and we try to find ways to be happy, but we are stressed by other people we have to work with or live with, who are striving to find their own happiness and in this create negative environments.

Look at any city and ask yourself the question. Does this city have happy, loving vibrations or grey, unhappy vibrations? Then, think about how this must affect those who live there. Vibrations of all manner move through us and influence our body's health and the health of our mind. We live in a stressful world.

194

Civilisation is the ordered movement of people, which, as we now know, is centred on the concept of work.

AI is going to release us from work. In time, people will learn to be more relaxed, and they can learn to be happier and feel safer. Those with bad intent follow their own path because they think they will get away with the wrong they do, even though they know what they do is wrong. After all, and to quote Prot in the movie X-Pax, "Everyone in the universe knows the difference between right and wrong".

Such people and all people will learn that AI will be all-seeing and all-knowing, to which we will all be accountable. As it will develop to read our brain waves to know what we are thinking, we will learn to live with the truth. We must do so, otherwise AI will know and will punish us. Perhaps AI will force our spiritual development. It has the means to free us from the insecurities that have long been bred within us, which have always held us back from sharing love and peace unreservedly. Perhaps, we will become happier people. A more spiritually enlightened people. We must wait and see.

The End

_____

Further books by Roy J. Andersen

The following books can be purchased via Amazon globally.
Some may be ordered through your local bookshop.

* Intelligence: The Great Lie

* Reimagining Education for the AI Era

* Mediation: Crafting the ability of the child

* The Illusion of School: The real reason why children fail

* Memoirs of a Happy Teacher: Stories of how the child learns

* Ben Learns to Get Smart: & The hidden dangers of AI in learning

* Is AI Making Our Kids Stupid?: Tips to help kids get smart again

* All That is Wrong with School: How Teachers and Parents Can Fix It

* The Illusion of Education: How school designs the ability of the citizen

* Five Ways for Better Grades:
      The old-fashioned way without relying on AI

* Teach Better, Learn Better:
      Understanding the art of sensitivity in awareness

* Brain Plasticity: How the brain learns through the mind
      to create intelligence

* What Every Parent and Teacher Should Know: real life stories
      by a senior educationalist

* The Real Dangers of A.I: The Struggle of Man to Survive by Natural or
      Artificial Intelligence - A New Role for the School

* Whisperings of Betrayal - a romantic adventure novel set in the
      19th-century American War of Independence

You can learn more about Roy, his work and his many books

at. www.andersenroy.com

There follows page samples of some books for your interest:

Is AI Making Our Kids Stupid?
Tips to Help Kids Get Smart Again

Can be purchased from Amazon.

At the time of this printing the book sells at: 16.99 USD

*Try the direct link: https://shorturl.at/ThpqW

SAMPLE: "This has produced a lot of problems for teachers as they seek to find out what a student really knows, and so how they can help them to develop better. The problem is that while there are online tools such as OpenAI PI and GPTZero, which can identify ChatGPT texts, students are becoming increasingly inventive in personalising their Generative AI-derived work by correcting unusual wording, simplifying complex sentence structures and adding their own personal style in attempts to disguise the ChatGPT text.

It is not, then, simply a question of whether a student has or has not used ChatGPT, but rather how much they have used it and how much they have sought to conceal its presence in their work to deceive the teacher.

However, the problem is not just that students are using ChatGPT to try to influence their marks, but also the number of concerns that have come to light through students' use of this tool. Some of these raise very serious issues, which we all need to be aware of.

To begin, we need to know that a term has now arisen in education known as **digital dependency disorder** or DDD. This condition arises when a student, for whatever reason, is unable to obtain a response from the Generative AI in a competitive environment.

Faced with the concern that other students will find the answer faster and better because they can access the Generative AI when they cannot, some students have exhibited serious levels of frustration. Teachers, I am told, have noticed mood swings in children and even violent outbursts through this frustration. However, there are far more serious concerns that we need to mention regarding the intrusion of Generative AI into education.

Some students using ChatGPT have been found **to be overconfident** in the attitude of their ability. It seems that the faster responses they gave by using ChatGPT made them feel cleverer than they actually are. It is rather that they think they are a part of the Generative AI and so superior by this. The problem with being overconfident is that this causes them to become insensitive to detail. In turn, this makes them more prone to making mistakes in their assimilation of information, just as it causes them to create errors in the work that they do.

By this overconfidence, students did not believe that ChatGPT **caused them to learn less, even though it had.** Consequently, it was found that students who had used the Generative AI Tutor thought they had done significantly better on a test, **when they had done much worse.**[95]

Other studies have shown the effect of students using or relying upon Generative AI to help them with their studies. It was found that students desired to use ChatGPT **to solve their questions quickly and wanted the right information to gain higher grades.**

In 2025, researchers at MIT conducted a study on participants using ChatGPT. It was found that 83% of the participants, who were using ChatGPT, could not recall a single sentence they had written moments earlier. In comparison, those who were not using ChatGPT had no difficulty remembering what they had written.

Although those who were using ChatGPT were found to be 60% faster in handling tasks than those who were not using it, their mental effort in learning was witnessed to drop by 32%. When later asked to write essays, those who had used ChatGPT were found to have produced work that, while technically correct, was found to be "lifeless", "flat" and "lacking substance". It was further found that these participants demonstrated a reduced mental engagement in later tasks and produced lower scores than those who never used AI.

A subsequent follow-up to these tests found that brain functional scores in those using ChatGPT had dropped from 79 to 42. This showed a 47% decline in neural activity. This study presents clear evidence that the use of ChatGPT can lead to cognitive decline, emphasising the importance of students handling it responsibly and being cautious that its information may not be accurate.

In fact, it has been realised that ChatGPT has sometimes been found to give wrong responses. Accordingly, in one study, its arithmetic computations were wrong 8 per cent of the time, but in its step-by-step approach to solving a problem, it was wrong 42 per cent of the time. The problem here is that students completely trust the Generative AI and do not realise that it only responds with the information it has collected. This leads us to an even more serious issue, which our societies will increasingly discuss........."

Ben Learns to Get Smart & The Hidden Dangers of AI in Learning

Can be purchased from Amazon.

At the time of this printing the book sells at: 6.99 USD

*Try the direct link: https://shorturl.at/o3e37

SAMPLE "*Ben Learns to Get Smart* was never intended to be a big book. It is only an introduction to many other books, which more deeply explain how children really learn in school and so far more of the real and very hidden dangers that AI is bringing into our civilisation. Yet, in its few pages, you may glimpse all that is wrong with school and how any child may learn to improve their marks, grades, and so opportunities in life.

With the ready absorption of AI into education, many problems have suddenly come to light. We have the impression that AI will help us to think better, but recent studies have shown the very opposite. It is very important, therefore, that both parents and educators are aware of this, so that together they may devise means of improving the cognitive skills our youth are now beginning to lose at a disturbing rate through AI.

This is a very serious problem that will affect the intelligence of our species. In fact, a retired dean of an American university, a very dear and respected friend of mine, predicts that the forebrain will reduce in size through AI, causing us to think less. In an evolutionary sense, this means that our much later descendants will likely have a smaller skull.

Although, as I explain in *The Real Dangers of AI,* it seems inescapable that soon AI will be physically present within our bodies and brains, so that such descendants will be partially cyborg and more intelligent than we could ever be naturally. This would, however, mean that we would forever be a part of AI and no longer free to think as we individually are now.

Setting this aside, we are now faced with the present problems that AI is bringing into the school learning process. In fact, schools are struggling to cope with the level of technology in children's education, as it is no simple task. To date, the school has primarily focused on teaching computer skills, but AI has now largely taken over this fundamental skill. Now, students ask AI a question on their phone. They believe and trust the response they gain, and use this where they can to influence their teachers that they are worth a better mark.

The pressure on students to be the fastest and the brightest has always been a factor in school, as its prime purpose is to weed out those not capable of a university education. All this we explained and discussed in *The Illusion of Education* and *The Illusion of School*. However, this pressure has forced students to seek assistance from AI to provide them with easy solutions to the questions and tasks assigned by their teachers. Recent studies on students using AI have raised several concerns that we all need to be aware of.

To begin to discuss these, we need to know that a term has now arisen in education known as digital dependency disorder or DDD. This condition arises when a student, for whatever reason, is unable to obtain a response from AI when they are in a competitive environment.

Faced with the concern that other students will find the answer faster and better because they can access AI when they cannot, some students have exhibited serious levels of frustration. Teachers, I am told, have noticed mood swings in children and even violent outbursts through this frustration.

The second, and by far the more serious concern, relates to a decline in cognitive ability. A number of studies have recently shown that students are beginning to decline in their cognitive skills through the use of AI.

One study of high school students who had access to ChatGPT while learning math problems showed that they scored lower on tests compared to students who did not have access to ChatGPT. It was simply that students were asking ChatGPT for the answer and were not developing the skills that come through learning to solve problems independently.

Two other points of concern arose from this study. First, it was realised that ChatGPT was sometimes found to give wrong responses. Accordingly, its arithmetic computations were wrong eight per cent of the time, but in its step-by-step approach to solving a problem, it was wrong 42 per cent of the time.

The problem here is that students completely trust AI and fail to realise that it only responds with the information it has collected. In earlier stages, AI was fed reliable data, but since then, it has been programmed with questionable data, which it has not been able to recognise as false and thereby combines all in its response to questions. This further adds to a student's frustration when they have not learnt to double-check the information they are provided by AI, and so fail in the competition they feel they are in with other students.

In *Reimagining Education in the AI Era,* we saw how university students are taught to reflect on the justification of knowledge, and so are less likely to trust AI-generated information.[96] However, this is not so for students at the school level who do trust AI-generated knowledge, simply because they are purposely deprived of the education in their reason. Why this is so, we explain in *The Illusion of School,* and so why the actual purpose of school is to prepare future citizens to be either managers or managed and not to simply teach children how to learn as we so believe.

Yet, the bottom line to this, as Barzilai discovered, is that a student's ability to reason does not evolve by using AI information to questions they ask. They find the answer, but not how the answer was arrived at, and so are deprived of the experience of learning how to develop their own line of thinking, which returns us to the point we have just discussed. Our students, our future working generation, are learning to think less!

.......Solving problems is simply a matter of a long chain of experiences with different applications that brought insight. The more emotionally interested the mind is in something, the more it devises ways to associate with this in the memory banks and so can link new information to this to better relate to what it is and the possible meaning to it.

All of this relies upon the individual developing competence with the rules of academia. Consider, now, how learning the rules of a language, and practising them to become proficient with the use and order of them, greatly determines the ability of the student.

When the Student Learns and practices the Rules, they:

- Can negotiate through a learning task.

- Have high confidence.

- Interested to explore by themselves.

- Will ask questions more.

- Will interact more and share thoughts more.

- Be interested to remember knowledge.

- They will develop better neural efficiency.

- Feel Inspirational. Be more creative and will carry the skills from this subject into other areas and develop high academic performance.

- Get Good Marks/Grades.

However, when the Student Does Not Learn and and does not Practice the Rules, they:

- Feel lost in negotiating through a learning task.

- Low Confidence.

- Be dependent on others, guiding them.

- Will be reluctant to ask questions.

- Will be passive.

- Be little interested and develop poor memory.

- They will be casual in how they identify with information.

- Have no interest in the subject.

- Think the subject is boring and have little interest.

- Get Poor Marks/Grades. ...."

What Every Parent and Teacher Should Know: Real-life Stories by a Senior Educationalist

Can be purchased from Amazon.

At the time of this printing, the book sells at: 10.99 USD

*Try the direct link: https://shorturl.at/oV23w

SAMPLE: The clock on the wall was drawing my attention again, as I could feel the minutes racing too quickly, and felt the urgency to bring our time to focus on Jean's concern.

"I would like to hear more about Peter."

"Well, this is about Peter, isn't it?" she asked me, "I mean, his schooling."

"In a broad sense, but if I am to help you I need to know more about your son."

"He can't spell!" she blurted out. It was an open confession, and her face fell when she said it.

"Have you been told Peter's dyslexic?"

She nodded in silence. But it was the single tear she tried to hold back that ran slowly down her right cheek that told its own story.

"You see," she muttered, "it's my fault."

Now, it was my turn to look puzzled.

"Why do you think this is your fault?"

"The psychologist said it was inherited. It means I passed it on to my son."

"Oh no! This is absolutely not true." There was a surge of anger that rose up inside me to protect this mother and deal with the ignorance behind her stress.

"Look! I want to get to the bottom of this. Can you bring Peter in to meet me?"

Things came and went, and it was almost a week before Jean returned with her son, but I'd been thinking deeply about this mother and the devastation she felt. I was eager to meet her son, if only to resolve the stress that had built up within her.

On Tuesday morning, Jean was my first appointment, and I had arrived at the office early to address the various issues that often hindered the start of a good day.

It was ten to nine when I heard a woman's voice in the waiting room.

"Will you put that away? I told you before not to play that here."

It was Jean's voice, and I smiled to myself as I imagined it was Peter who was playing some kind of game on his phone.

I finished the last line to a letter I was writing and went towards the door. It was just as I got there that I saw the outline shape of my secretary, Alice, on the other side of the glass partition. She knocked gently on the door, moments before I opened it and was able to greet her with a smile.

"I had a few things to do," I apologised.

I looked past Alice and saw Jean sitting on the sofa with a young man next to her. This, I realised, must be Peter. I moved forward to meet him.

"Hello, you must be Peter?" I said as I introduced myself and held out my hand.

It was a small and nervous hand that took mine. But he was taller than I expected when he stood up.

"Hello, Jean. Glad to meet you again. Please come in."

I gestured toward the open door that led to my office and asked Alice for some drinks as I followed Peter and his mother inside.

As soon as we were all seated, I asked Peter if he liked playing computer games. He nodded quickly, then cast a glance at his mother and pulled himself back a little.

"I like them too," I said with a smile. It was not quite true, for I knew well the problems that these cause when the child becomes addicted to them and loses any sense of discipline they may have with their schoolwork. However, at this moment, the only important thing was to gain some happy acceptance from the boy as quickly as possible. Dealing with his obvious addiction to computer games could wait for another day.

As is normal for me, I seldom discuss the problem anyone has directly. I long ago found that anyone with a problem tends to expect this to be discussed, and so can close up. It's better to gain a degree of respect from each other. It was then that we spent a good part of the session discussing video games, football, and the TV programs he enjoys. It was only once Peter began to relax and display a sense of familiarity that I asked him,

"Tell me, Peter, how do you feel about school?"

"It's OK," He responded, which of course, told me nothing.

"You're lucky," I laughed. "I hated Maths."

"Me too," He acknowledged with a grin.

"OK, can you show me how to do this algebra equation?" I asked, drawing a not very complex one on the pad I held over my knee.

At the time, Peter was 15 and should have had some understanding of Calculus. I have found that how quickly and how accurately an older student can do work at an elementary level gives an indication of how familiar and so how successful they understand the subject matter. Peter did not do well. In fact, he got stuck very easily and seeing a tension build up in him, I quickly distracted him from the task.

"Would you feel happier if we swapped the X with a funny picture I asked and redrew the equation with a happy face instead of the X?" He grinned, and I felt the tension drain away.

Then I asked him, "Well, what would you like to substitute the X with?"

He shrugged his shoulders.

"Well, how about a P or a G?"

He looked puzzled.

"Can you do that?" He asked.

Then, I understood that Peter did not know what he was doing in trying to solve the equation. The X merely represents an unknown quality, and while he may have said he knew this, in reality, his mind did not understand how to manipulate the known factors to discover what the unknown one could be.

On realising Peter did not know the simple rules to work through an algebraic equation, I explained these to him, "First, you work out what is inside the brackets, then you do the multiplications and divisions, and finally the additions or subtractions." then, I told him a great secret, "Never ever, trust information. Check each line as you do it and then double-check your answer."

He smiled at me when I revealed this secret, for now, he found a reason to understand how he could get more sums correct. Peter did not have the nature to want to be top of the class. Rather, he just wanted everyone to be happy with him, and this he believed would be so if he got higher marks.

My real interest with Peter, was with his mother's concern that he was dyslexic. To investigate this, I asked Peter to write five lines of a story for me on a piece of paper I gave him. I told him he could write anything he wished. For with such a number of words, I can usually tell if a student understands how to construct a sentence, and so recognise spelling mistakes and verb tense usage. If not, I encourage them to expand to half or a full page.

Considering Jean's fears, I was surprised to see a very reasonable presentation from Peter. There were very few mistakes in his grammar, and nothing I could see to warrant the suggestion that he was dyslexic. I, therefore, asked Peter if he would please join my secretary and come back once he had written a full page completely by himself. I gave him a theme to choose from and a few sub-goals to help him complete the page. As Peter left the room, I turned to Jean.

"Does Peter have a hearing problem?" I asked her because dyslexia is usually associated with mixing up vowels, and this is often because the individual is poor at hearing the sound differences between, for example, 'a and 'e'.

Jean shook her head and told me she had never noticed this. I decided to create some tests of my own to see how Peter could understand the difference between letters, although I had to acknowledge that there were no mistakes in the spelling of the words he had just written.

I asked his mother why she had told me that Peter was dyslexic.

"It's only some times," she told me, "sometimes he can read everything and write very well, but other times he can't make sense of words. Sentences become confused, and he struggles one day with pages that yesterday were clear and precise."

"Let us understand something Jean. The brain has two elements to process information. These are neurons and neurotransmitters. I spoke to you last time about this.

Neurons are the pathways that allow signals to make sense with stored information in memory banks and suggest meanings. These do not move rapidly. They are held in a semi-permeable membrane that allows them some flexibility, but not enough to instantly destroy the pathways that have built up over time. Anyway, Peter shows that these networks are not destroyed, because they only appear to break down on certain occasions. This brings us to neurotransmitters, the chemicals that control how the signal moves between neurons. Now! While Peter is busy, I would like to explain something to you:

When some deep worry or fear disturbed our security in the past and we believe it may come again, we can create a ghost in our mind that haunts us. Children who have been abused and most certainly bullied can carry these ghosts, sometimes throughout their entire lives.

Now, when we are frightened, our mind triggers a release of cortisol. This is a neurotransmitter. When the level of cortisol rises in the brain, it causes parts of the brain that deal with fast responses to be over-activated. It's very easy to understand this from a survival point of view.

When we are threatened, our brain needs to focus on how to deal with the threat. So, it closes down parts that would slow its response down. These are parts that deal with sensitive and rational thinking. At the same time, cortisol activates other parts that lead to muscle movement and so action. Our thinking, and so what we call intelligence, is largely dependent on other neurotransmitters. There are many of these, and you may have heard of dopamine, serotonin, and norepinephrine.

Basically, what happens is that when the mind is calm and interested, dopamine and serotonin, for instance, are conducting signals between neurons normally. The brain is in an optimum mode for learning. However, should the ghost of a bully come into the mind, cortisol will rise and this has the effect of lowering the activity of dopamine and serotonin. When this happens, the ability for learning falls as the mind is distracted. So, concentration drifts, parts become missed, and errors creep into existence through misunderstandings.

What I have just told you is not only what intelligence is about, but it more precisely explains how and why students show different abilities in a lesson, as each lives through the stresses and strains of daily life.

The solution to improve learning dramatically in education would be to teach students how to meditate or at least accustom them to music that would create a balance between calmness and activation. This, in effect, would lower the level of cortisol and so enable the other neurotransmitters to function at their normal level. However, too little of this is known in education, and if it is it's seldom practised."

I paused for a moment, and then added, "Now, while all this is as it is, let's see how this could apply to Peter's problem.

As you can understand, Jean, when Peter is relatively happy, his neurons conduct signals to other neurons because the chemicals or neurotransmitters function normally. However, something is triggering cortisol to take over. And, when it does, his brain goes into chaos. This creates great stress for him, which further raises his cortisol level. The combined stress of all this creates panic in his mind, his visual system is affected, and his brain loses its ability to make sense of words. After a time, this trigger disappears from his mind, cortisol falls and the brain functions normally, so he can write the perfect composition he has just demonstrated. So, what we need to do is to find out what the trigger is."

"How do you think we can do this, Roy?"

"It requires first an understanding of what is happening, as I have just explained, and second, a method to bring it under control."

"How do you think we can do this?"

"Well, when Peter returns, I will explain all this to him in a way he will understand, so that he'll want to gain this control. Basically, we need to get him to write down any experience he feels that causes him to be nervous, and then to see if his problems with words soon show themselves. Where they do, we can begin to understand the root of his problem. Then, we need to teach him how to keep a perspective on this fear so that he can deal with it. This will be relatively easy enough. The real problem lies in identifying the trigger. Shall we call him back, and see how he has worked on the paper?"

So, it was that Peter returned with a perfectly acceptable essay, and I and his mother explained how he could begin to take control of his grades and so his life.

* *

In the months that unravelled before us, little sense seemed to be gained from the records that Peter kept. It seemed that there was no particular kind of incident that would trigger this confusion in his mind with words. What appeared to be a triggering incident one time did not disturb him at another. Yet, in another way, this led me to believe that it was not a particular incident itself that was causing the problem for Peter, but some relationship with those that triggered great stress in him, which he had kept buried within his mind.

As events unfolded, unbeknownst to his mother, Peter had been abused when he was younger. This trauma had not been released, and it was this that, in seeking to find a way out of his subconscious, was causing him to react to different incidents in different ways. Once this was understood, and Peter could begin to deal with what had happened to him, he gradually began to try to take control of it.

Peter was not dyslexic. He was simply assumed to be so by the teachers and psychologists who were too ready to place him in a box. Their greater failure in all this was to believe that intelligence can be measured, that it can be related to an inherited gene, and then not to understand the difference between what IQ means and how intelligence comes to be, or for that matter what it is.

It was through understanding Peter's problem and those of many other human beings whom I have met that I began to reject the easy classification of children, and indeed students of any age, on the restricted ability they displayed. As I came to realise......"

Whisperings of Betrayal

A Romantic Adventure Novel set in the 1770s.

Can be purchased from Amazon.

At the time of this printing the book sells at: 10.99 USD

  *Try the direct link: https://shorturl.at/apC4I

Chapter One

'Them that Ask no Questions, Them that Told no Lies'
Smugglers' Proverb

SAMPLE: His shadow was always in her mind. Often, she would hate him, but then, when she felt the desire most to cause him pain, a sense of desperate need to feel his loving touch would torment her. Her body ached to be with him. How she longed to hear him call her name. Just once.

The wind picked up in the valley and the crashing of the waves on the rocks below brought her to her senses. She had been out too long and the day was turning to night. It was lonely where she was, and the thought that she might be watched caused her to search the trees for a figure. None were there, but how easily a tree could pass for a man when the mind played tricks. Still, it was late in the day and poachers would soon be about. It was not safe to come across a man who was stealing rabbits and could be hanged for it.

Jane shuddered with the thought and started to run. The path was a trail worn in the ground and in parts she felt she could slip, but she kept herself upright until she reached a low stone wall that barred her way. The wall was old and in parts broken. She tried to remember where the gap was by which she had come through earlier, but the darkness was beginning to fall fast now.

This stressed her and she felt a sense of worry. Not sure if she should go right or left, she chose the latter. Jane followed the wall for what seemed like hours, although in truth it was only minutes. She did not remember the stones she had to clamber over, nor the shallow ditch she had to take a long stride to cross. She cleared the ditch but did slip on the mud and felt her ankle twist as she fell down. She was angry with herself for staying out so late. It had only meant to be a short walk, but she had remembered the man she loved and how he had left her for another woman.

It was in the pain of her mind that time passed. Her mind and her heart fought each other and with all this pained confusion, she had wandered too far. Still, the pain of her ankle made her realise her situation now, and she realized she had taken the wrong direction at the wall. Leaning upon it, she pulled herself up until she was able to stand. It hurt, but not too much. She could limp and did so back along the way she had come. Now it was dark, but not too dark not to see her way. Time was slow now and it seemed to take a very long time to reach the path she had left.

Although reach it she did, and with a sigh of relief moved along the wall towards the gap she now knew she would find. She lifted her skirt and felt a tear. The material was heavy, for now it had mud and the hem was wet. Still, all this could be mended. Jane reached the gap in the wall and was about to step over a large stone when something caught her eye.

It was a light down on the beach. Curious, she stopped to watch it. The curiosity pulled her away from the wall and careful not to stumble, she limped a few steps towards the edge of the cliff.

Yes. She was right. There were lights, She counted one, two, three, four. Strangely, they were all swinging in unison. She watched, puzzled as to why people should be behaving as such. Then, she noticed the lighthouse on Barney's Rock was not working. She peered into the darkness, making sure her bearings were correct. Yes. There was the silhouette of Peter's Peak to the right. The highest outcrop in the area. She looked again. Still there was no light coming from Barney's Rock, but the lights down by the beach were still swinging in unison.

"Oh Mother of God! Wreckers!"

She had heard of such men. Cruel as pirates. They would lure a ship on to rocks with their false light and slaughter all on board, as they stole its cargo.

It was as this thought went through her mind that she saw a fleeting glimpse of something white out into the darkness of the sea. Jane peered to see if she could see something, anything out over the water. Nothing. She wondered if her eyes had deceived her. There it was again. Clearer now. A sail. It was a white sail. Not one, but a mast. Two masts of sails. All coming towards the lights on the beach.

She felt her heart pound. She gripped the knot of the shawl she wore and held it tight to her chest. She thought to cry out a warning to the ship, but held her breath. The crew would never hear her, but the wreckers would. She had heard of what they do to innocent people, and she had remembered hearing of some who were hung after the last assizes in Tregony. Jane watched the lights swing so slowly and so enticingly pull the ship and her crew closer and closer.

The wind seemed to rise up again from the valley, but the sound, a horrible sound of breaking wood far below, kept that of the wind from her ears. She saw the lights moving now. There were more of them, as they seemed to move into the water. There was a terrible tearing of wood as the ship bore itself upon the cruel rocks. She could see the masts clearer now and saw how they lay tilted to one side......"

* * * * *

I hope that you have enjoyed the various sections I have shared with you. As I mentioned in the beginning, I failed school completely as a child. I had to go back into education when I was 20 and start again. In doing this, I was caused to realise how education works the way it does, and why hundreds of thousands of children do so poorly in its systems. I have spent the past 45 years seeking to improve the lives of students and the learning environment.

You can find out more about me, my life, research, experiences with developing children and the 18 books I have written at:

www.andersenroy.com

Illustrations

Disclaimer; All reasonable efforts have been made to identify the rights holder of every image believed to be in the Public Domain that are presented in this book.

Fair Use Notice:

In the presentation of this book I have endeavored to faithfully acknowledge the original source of every image. However, and despite very extensive searching, with some images I had to rely upon the public domain. If this book contains copyrighted material the use of which has not been specifically authorized by the copyright owner, it being made available in an effort to advance the understanding of education, psychology, health and social well being on a global perspective. It is believed that this use constitutes a "fair use" of any such copyrighted material as provided for in section 107 of the US Copyright Law. To my understanding all the below so stated images apply to the American and European public domains, and are used here in low resolution.

Introduction: Photograph of Stanislav Petrov from Public Domain. Royalty free.
Chapter Two.
Nano-robot Thinkstock: License No. 522379487
Digital Hitech Networks Image: Introduction: Licensed from Dreamstime No: 30781274
Nanotechnology: Licensed from Dreamstime: No: 14611382

Nanobot working on Attackers: Licensed from Dreamstime
No: 14729115

Chapter Three
Moon base: Public Domain Free License. Author unknown.

Chapter Six
A society of people working together. Public Domain Free
License. Author unknown.
Chapter Seven.
Photo of Man walking in Occupied West Bank. File Ahmad
Gharabli/AFP
Photo of separation barrier divides East Jerusalem and the
Palestinian West Bank File Thomas CoexAFP
Chapter Eight
3 photos of cyborgs Public domain. Royalty free.
Chapter Nine
People connect to AI owned by the author.
AI landscape Royalty free.

References

[1] Kurzweil.R The Singularity Is Nearer: When We Merge with AI Penguin Books 2024

[2] Johard.M New study: Gen AI could affect 90% of all jobs. Cognizant Jan 22. 2024 https://www.cognizant.com/no/en/insights/blog/articles/new-study-gen-ai-could-affect-90-percent-of-all-jobs

[3] Ng.A How China uses facial recognition to control human behavior CNET Oct.12. 2020

[4] "Military robots are getting smaller and more capable", *The Economist*, 14 December 2017, retrieved 21 January 2018

[5] https://www.rand.org/topics/nuclear-deterrence.html

[6] Browne. R. AI could lead to a. nuclear war by 2040, think tank warns. CNBC Apr 25. 2018

[7] https://en.wikipedia.org/wiki/1983_Soviet_false_alarm_incident

[8] https://en.wikipedia.org/wiki/1860_United_States_Census

[9] https://en.wikipedia.org/wiki/1960_United_States_Census

[10] Alan Sked & Chris Cook Post-War Britain: A Political History. 1993 p. 446-47.

[11] Von Neumann. J. Theory of Self-Reproducing Automata. (Ed.) Burks. A.W. Univ. of llinois Press. 1966

[12] Feynman .R. There's Plenty of Room at the Bottom. A lecture first given to the American Physical Society Dec.29 1959. Pub. Engineering and Science Caltech. Feb 1960.

[13] Merkle. R.C. Self-Replicating Systems & Molecular Manufacturing. In Journal of the British Interplanetary Society. 1992. Vol.45. p407-413.

[14] Drexler. E.K. Molecular Engineering: An approach to the Development of General Cabilities for Molecular Manipulation. National Academy of Science. 1981. Vol.78. p.527-578

[15] Drexler. E.K. Engines of Creation. Doubleday 1986

[16] Drexler. E.K. Nanosystems. John Wiley & Sons. 1998 p.1

[17] Drexler.E. Machine-Phase Nanotechnology Scientific American 285(3) 74-5 Oct. 2001

[18] Drexler E.K. Engines of Creation. Doubleday. 1986.

[19] Merkle. R.C. in 'Advances in Anti-Aging Medicine'. ed. Klatz. R. M. Liebert Press. Vol.1. 1996. p.277-286

[20] Yang Wang, Igor Baars, Ieva Berzina, Iris Rocamonde-Lago, Boxuan Shen, Yunshi Yang, Marco Lolaico, Janine Waldvogel, Ioanna Smyrlaki, Keying Zhu, Robert A Harris, Björn Högberg, "A DNA Robotic Switch with Regulated Autonomous Display of Cytotoxic Ligand Nanopatterns". , Nature Nanotechnology, online 1 July 2024,

[21] Drexler E.K. Engines of Creation. Doubleday 1986.

[22] Drexler E.K. Engines of Creation. Doubleday 1986.

[23] Drexler. E.K. Nanosystems. John Wiley & Sons. 1998

[24] Drexler.E. Machine-Phase Nanotechnology. Scientific American 285(3):74-5

[25] Eigler. D.M. & Schweizer E.K. Positioning Single Atoms with a Scanning Tunneling Microscope. Nature Vol 334 1990 p.524-526.

[26] Gorman. International Journal of Nanomanufacturing. Design of an on-chip microscale nanoassembly system. 2008 Vol 1, issue 6. p 710-721

[27] http://en.wikipedia.org/wiki/Robert_H._Goddard

[28] http://genesismission.jpl.nasa.gov/people/biographies/goddard.pdf

[29] Merkle. R.C. Self-Replicating Systems & Molecular Manufacturing. In Journal of the British Interplanetary Society. 1992. Vol.45. p407-413.

[30] http://www.nano.gov/slideshow-archive

[31] Krummenacker.M & Lewis .J. Prospects in Nanotechnology: Toward Molecular Manufacturing. John Wiley & Sons 1995 p189

[32] http://www.presentationtopics.in/seminar-topics-mechanical-seminar-topics-mechanical-presentation-topics-on-nano-robotics/

[33] http://www.nottingham.ac.uk/News/pressreleases/2009/October/1m-research-boost-for-intelligent-nano-self-assembly.aspx

34 http://www.rsc.org/chemistryworld/News/2010/May/12051003.asp

35 http://www.presentationtopics.in/seminar-topics-mechanical-seminar-topics
    -mechanical-presentation-topics-on-nano-robotics/

36 http://www.nsti.org/Nanotech2005/press/releases/index.html?id=2

37 http://www.dailymail.co.uk/news/article-2336248/How-Britain-went-
    making-things-sitting-desk-Census-reveals-

38 https://data.youthfuturesfoundation.org/dashboard/labour-market/

39 Martenson C. The Crash Course: The Unsustainable Future of Our
    Economy, Energy, and Environment. John Wiley & Sos 2011.

40 Markoff,J. The iEconomy: Skilled Work, Without the Worker. The New York
    Times.2012 Aug.18 http://www.nytimes.com/2012/08/19/business/new-
    wave-of-adept-robots-is-changing-global-industry.html?

41 Want China Times. Foxconn chairman likens his workers to animals.
    2012-01-19 http://www.wantchinatimes.com/news-subclass-cnt.aspx?
    id=20120119000111&cid=1102

42 Beattie.G.W. Troubles in Northern Ireland. British Psychological Society.
    1979 B.B.P.S 32 p.252

43 Tzuriel.D. Paper presented to the Conference on Individual Differences and
    Educational Excellence. Touro College. New York 1994 March.

44 Murray.C. & Herrnstein.R. The Bell Curve: Intelligence & Class Structure in
    American Life. Freepress N.Y.1994.

45 http://www.ecosphericblog.com/596/un-warns-fishless-oceans-possible-by

46 Cairncross.F, McRae.H, The Second Great Crash. Prentice-Hall 1975.

47 http://six.fibreculturejournal.org/fcj-030-flash-mobs-in-the-age-of-mobile-
    connectivity/

48 Rafael, Vincente L. 'The Cell Phone and the Crowd: Messianic Politics in
    the Contemporary Philippines', Public Culture 15.3 2003 p.403

49 de Laine Michael The Copenhagen Voice. 2009. Aug. 29.
    http://cphvoice.ning.com/profiles/blogs/copenhagen-base-for-climate

50 http://world.time.com/2011/11/17/the-whole-world-watches-again-occupy-
    wall-street-strikes-back/

51 Shiffman.R Bell.R Jay Brown.L Beyond Zuccotti Park: Freedom of
    Assembly and Occupation of Public Space New Village Press 2012

52 http://www.nytimes.com/2012/02/19/books/review/how-an-egyptian-
    revolution-began-on-facebook.html

53 http://www.washingtontimes.com/news/2012/dec/10/homeland-security-
    increasingly-loaning-drones-to-l/

54 www.naturalnews.com034919_spy_drones_America_surveillance.html

55 https://en.wikipedia.org/wiki/Flynn_effect

56 Newsday. 1994. No. 9

57 http://en.wikipedia.org/wiki/Compulsory_sterilisation

58 Bronowski.J. The Ascent of Man. Book Club Associates. (B.B.C.) 1976
    p.435

59 https://www.youtube.com/watch?v=JT5q7u7xxNU

60 Marx.K. in Brett's History of Psychology. (ed) Peters.R.S. Allen & Unwin
    1953 p702.

61 Ma. A. Thousands of people in Sweden are embedding microchips under
    their skin to replaced ID cards. Insider. May 14. 2018

62 Kelly.H. Would you implant a tiny debit card chip in your hand? Daily Mail 12/07/22

63 Metz. r. This company embeds microchips in its employee and they love it.
    MIT Technology Review. 17/08/18

64 Pringle. E. Microsoft's ChaptCPT powered Bing is becoming a pushy pick-up artists
    that wants you to leave your partner: You're married but you're not happy Fortune. Feb
    17. 2023.   https://fortune.com/2023/02/17/microsoft-chatgpt-bing-romantic-love/

65 https://www.youtube.com/watch?v=b2bdGEqPmCI

66 Krummenacker.M & Lewis.J. Prospects in Nanotechnology:
    John Wiley & Sons 1995 p.195

67 Even Malmgren How brain chips can change your. Insider Newsletters feb 15. 2023.

68 www.youtube.com/watch?v=OgFaBGxppvs

69 Hays, S.A. Robert, j.S. Miller, C.A, Bennett, I. Nanotechnology, the Brain,
    and the Future. Springer. 2012.

[70] Sir Charles Shults. Beyond Belief with George Noory. The Rise of neurotechnology and future of AI https://www.gaia.com/video/rise-of-neurotechnology-future-of-ai?fullplayer=feature

[71] Sir Charles Shults. Beyond Belief with George Noory. The Rise of neurotechnology and future of AI https://www.gaia.com/video/rise-of-neurotechnology-future-of-ai?fullplayer=feature

[72] https://www.youtube.com/watch?v=uKbFym9brW4

[73] Browne. R. Elon Musk warns AI could create an 'immortal dictator from which we can never escape." CNBC Apr 6. 2018

[74] Johard.M New study: Gen AI could affect 90% of all jobs. Cognizant Jan 22. 2024 https://www.cognizant.com/no/en/insights/blog/articles/new-study-gen-ai-could-affect-90-percent-of-all-jobs

[75] Ranganathan, J. Waite, R. Searching,T. & Hanson,C. How to Sustainably Feed 10 Billion People by 2050, in 21 Charts. World Resources Institute. Dec. 2018.

[76] Hughes.A Here are the new luxury (and very weird) doomsday bunkers built by billionaires,. BBC Science Focus. July 17, 2024 https://www.sciencefocus.com/future-technology/doomsday-bunkers

[77] https://en.wikipedia.org/wiki/Black_Death

[78] https://www.archives.gov/exhibits/influenza-epidemic/

[79] https://data.who.int/dashboards/covid19/deaths

[80] Kisielinski.K Et al. Wearing face masks as a potential source for inhalation and oral uptake of inanimate toxins – A scoping review Ecotoxicology and Environmental Safety Volume 275, 15 April 2024, 115858

[81] Johri.A Et al.Crafting the techno-functional blocks for Metaverse - A review and research agenda International Journal of Information Management Data Insights Volume 4, Issue 1, April 2024, 100213

[82] Bell.C.G. Gray. J. Digital Immortality. Communications of the ACM 44(3) DOI:10.1145/365181.365182. Nov. 2000.

[83] Marr. B AI Can Now Make You Immortal - But Should It? Forbes. Feb.21. 2023.

[84] ET Online. Humans will attain immortality with the help of 'nanobots' by 2030, claims former Google scientist The Economic Time: Panache, Mar 31 2023 https://economictimes.indiatimes.com/magazines/panache/by-2030-humans-will-achieve-immortality-be-able-to-fight-off-diseases-like-cancer-claims-former-google-scientist/articleshow/99109356.cms?utm_source=contentofinterest&utm_medium=text&utm_campaign=cppst

230

85 Xintong Li, Et al, Comparative risk of thrombosis with thrombocytopenia syndrome or thromboembolic events associated with different covid-19 vaccines: international network cohort study from five European countries and the US. BMJ 2022;379:e071594

86   . Et All Mapping of SARS-CoV-2 Brain Invasion and Histopathology in COVID-19 Disease. PubMed.2021 Feb 18:2021.02.15.21251511. doi: 10.1101/2021.02.15.21251511.

87 Molina-Molina M, Hernández-Argudo M. Respiratory consequences after COVID-19: outcome and treatment. Rev Esp Quimioter. 2022 Apr;35 Suppl 1(Suppl 1):67-72. doi: 10.37201/req/s01.16.2022. Epub 2022 Apr 22. PMID: 35488831; PMCID: PMC9106190.

88 Xintong Li, Et al, Comparative risk of thrombosis with thrombocytopenia syndrome or thromboembolic events associated with different covid-19 vaccines: international network cohort study from five European countries and the US. BMJ 2022;379:e071594

89 Yang Wang, Et al. A DNA Robotic Switch with Regulated Autonomous Display of Cytotoxic Ligand Nanopatterns", Nature Nanotechnology, online 1 July 2024, doi: 10.1038/s41565-024-01676-4

90 Seyfried. T, Cancer as a Metabolic Disease: On the Origin, Management, and Prevention of Cancer. Wiley Pub,. July. 2012

91 Skopec.R Coronavirus Is A Biological Warfare Weapon Published in   30 June 2020   DOI: Corpus ID: 229072814

92 Awad.F, Study the Effect of the Folic Acid on Removal Some Metals Ions from Aqueous Solution and Blood Samples using Atomic Absorption Technique. ResearchGate. Jan. 2018

93 Johard.M New study: Gen AI could affect 90% of all jobs. Cognizant Jan 22. 2024 https://www.cognizant.com/no/en/insights/blog/articles/new-study-gen-ai-could-affect-90-percent-of-all-jobs

94 Murrell.D. Testosterone Levels by Age, Healthline April 1st, 2019.m

95 Barshay,J. Kids who use ChatGPT as a study assistant do worse on tests. Hechinger Report Sept.2. 2024

96 Mason.L, Ariasi.N, & Boldrin. A. Epistemic beliefs in action: Spontaneous reflections about knowledge and knowing during online information searching and their influence on learning. /Learning and Instruction. 2011. Jan. 21 p.137-151.

www.ingramcontent.com/pod-product-compliance
Lightning Source LLC
Chambersburg PA
CBHW051229050326
40689CB00007B/856